Libby Moore

GCSE AQA A
Religious Studies

The more practice you can get for the AQA A Christianity & Islam options, the better. That's where this CGP book comes in...

It contains hundreds of realistic questions covering every topic you'll need to know, including beliefs, teachings and practices. We've also added lots of practice for the eight thematic studies, as well as sample answers.

You'll find answers and mark schemes at the back, along with handy tips to help you pick up top marks. Brilliant!

Exam Practice Workbook

Contents

✓ Use the tick boxes to check off the topics you've completed.

Getting Started

How to Use this Book .... 1 ☐
Exam Breakdown .... 2 ☐

Component 1: The Study of Religions: Beliefs, Teachings and Practices

Beliefs, Teachings and Practices — Christianity and Catholic Christianity

The Nature of God .... 3 ☐
Creation .... 4 ☐
Evil and Suffering .... 5 ☐
The Afterlife .... 6 ☐
Jesus Christ and Salvation .... 7 ☐
Worship and Prayer .... 9 ☐
The Sacraments .... 11 ☐
Pilgrimage .... 13 ☐
Christmas and Easter .... 14 ☐
The Work of the Church .... 15 ☐

Beliefs, Teachings and Practices — Islam

Key Beliefs in Islam .... 17 ☐
Authority .... 19 ☐
Life after Death .... 21 ☐
Worship .... 22 ☐
Duties .... 23 ☐
Festivals .... 25 ☐

Component 2: Thematic Studies

Theme A — Relationships and Families

Sexuality and Sexual Relationships .... 26 ☐
Marriage and Divorce .... 27 ☐
Families .... 29 ☐
Gender Equality .... 30 ☐

Theme B — Religion and Life

The Universe and the Environment .... 31 ☐
Abortion and Euthanasia .... 33 ☐
The Afterlife .... 35 ☐

Theme C — The Existence of God and Revelation
Design and Causation..36
Miracles and Revelation..37
Arguments Against the Existence of God..40

Theme D — Religion, Peace and Conflict
Peace and Conflict..41
Weapons of Mass Destruction..43
Peacemaking...44

Theme E — Religion, Crime and Punishment
Law, Crime and Forgiveness...45
Punishment and the Death Penalty...47

Theme F — Religion, Human Rights and Social Justice
Attitudes to Equality...49
Human Rights and Freedom of Belief...51
Social Justice, Wealth and Poverty...52

Theme G — St Mark's Gospel: the Life of Jesus
The Start of Jesus's Ministry...54
Jesus's Miracles...55
The Later Ministry of Jesus...56
The Final Days in Jerusalem...58

Theme H — St Mark's Gospel as a Source of Spiritual Truths
The Kingdom of God...60
People Disregarded by Society...62
Faith and Discipleship...64

Marking Guidance and Practice
2 Mark Questions...66
4 Mark Questions...68
5 Mark Questions...70
12 Mark Questions...72

Answers..75

Published by CGP

<u>Editors</u>: Emma Crighton, Emma Duffee, Hannah Lawson, Jack Simm

<u>Contributors</u>: Helen Norris, Rebecca Tate, Ben Wallace

<u>Proofreading</u>: Aimee Ashurst

ISBN: 978 1 83774 147 2

With thanks to Jade Sim for the copyright research.

Sacred Text References

References from the Bible always go in the order: Book Chapter:Verse(s). So whenever you see something like: Genesis 1:14, it means it's from the book of Genesis, Chapter 1, verse 14.

Similarly, references from the Qur'an are shown with the Surah (Chapter) followed by the Ayah (Verse).

For all collections of hadith, we've used the English referencing system.
This gives the book number followed by the hadith number, e.g. Sahih al-Bukhari 1:3.

Scripture quotations [marked NIV] taken from the Holy Bible,
New International Version Anglicised Copyright © 1979, 1984, 2011 Biblica.
Used by permission of Hodder & Stoughton Ltd, an Hachette UK company.
All rights reserved.

'NIV' is a registered trademark of Biblica UK trademark number 1448790.

Quotes from the Quran © The Clear Quran® – The Clear Quran is a registered trademark of Al-Furqaan Foundation.
Translated by – Dr. Mustafa Khattab
Published by – The Book of Signs Foundation or Furqaan Institute of Quranic Education, both divisions of Al-Furqaan Foundation
www.theclearquran.org

Catechism of the Catholic Church quotes © Dicastero per la Comunicazione-Libreria Editrice Vaticana

Quote on page 88 from Islam and the West: A Rational Perspective by Mohammed Jabbar,
published by Mereo Books, an imprint of Memoir Publishing 2014.

Every effort has been made to locate copyright holders and obtain permission to reproduce sources. For those sources where it has been difficult to trace the originator of the work, we would be grateful for information. If any copyright holder would like us to make an amendment to the acknowledgements, please notify us and we will gladly update the book at the next reprint. Thank you.

Printed by Elanders Ltd, Newcastle upon Tyne
Clipart from Corel®

Based on the classic CGP style created by Richard Parsons.

Text, design, layout and original illustrations © Coordination Group Publications Ltd. (CGP) 2024
All rights reserved.

Photocopying this book is not permitted, even if you have a CLA licence.
Extra copies are available from CGP with next day delivery • 0800 1712 712 • www.cgpbooks.co.uk

Getting Started

How to Use this Book

- Hold the book upright, approximately 50 cm from your face, ensuring that the text looks like this, not sıɥʇ. Alternatively, place the book on a horizontal surface (e.g. a table or desk) and sit adjacent to the book, at a distance which doesn't make the text too small to read.
- In case of emergency, press the two halves of the book together firmly in order to close.
- Before attempting to use this book, familiarise yourself with the following safety information:

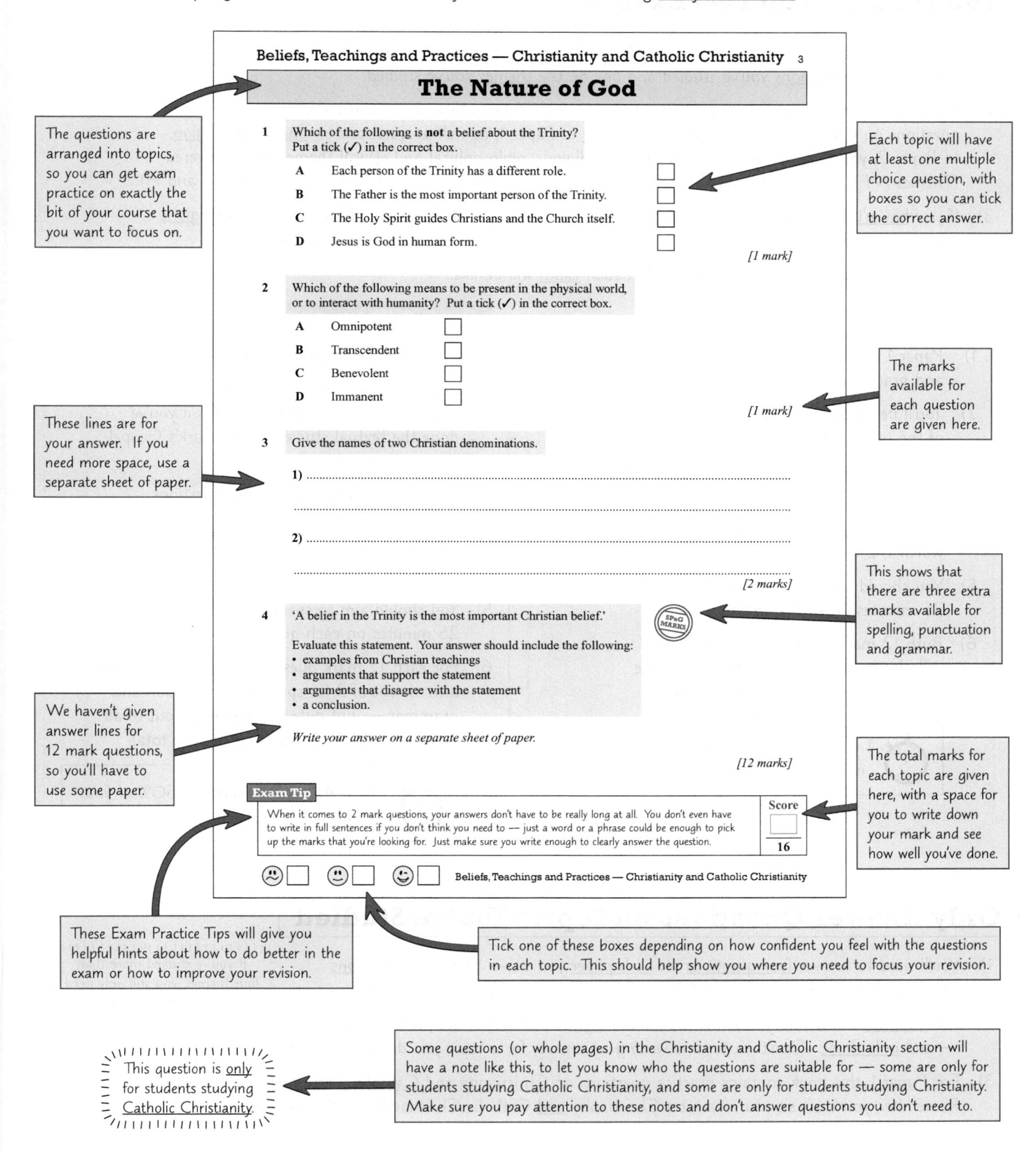

Beliefs, Teachings and Practices — Christianity and Catholic Christianity

The Nature of God

The questions are arranged into topics, so you can get exam practice on exactly the bit of your course that you want to focus on.

Each topic will have at least one multiple choice question, with boxes so you can tick the correct answer.

1 Which of the following is **not** a belief about the Trinity? Put a tick (✓) in the correct box.

A Each person of the Trinity has a different role. ☐
B The Father is the most important person of the Trinity. ☐
C The Holy Spirit guides Christians and the Church itself. ☐
D Jesus is God in human form. ☐

[1 mark]

2 Which of the following means to be present in the physical world, or to interact with humanity? Put a tick (✓) in the correct box.

A Omnipotent ☐
B Transcendent ☐
C Benevolent ☐
D Immanent ☐

[1 mark]

The marks available for each question are given here.

These lines are for your answer. If you need more space, use a separate sheet of paper.

3 Give the names of two Christian denominations.

1) ....

2) ....

[2 marks]

4 'A belief in the Trinity is the most important Christian belief.'

(SPaG MARKS)

Evaluate this statement. Your answer should include the following:
- examples from Christian teachings
- arguments that support the statement
- arguments that disagree with the statement
- a conclusion.

Write your answer on a separate sheet of paper.

This shows that there are three extra marks available for spelling, punctuation and grammar.

[12 marks]

We haven't given answer lines for 12 mark questions, so you'll have to use some paper.

Exam Tip
When it comes to 2 mark questions, your answers don't have to be really long at all. You don't even have to write in full sentences if you don't think you need to — just a word or a phrase could be enough to pick up the marks that you're looking for. Just make sure you write enough to clearly answer the question.

Score: 16

The total marks for each topic are given here, with a space for you to write down your mark and see how well you've done.

☹ ☐ 😐 ☐ ☺ ☐   Beliefs, Teachings and Practices — Christianity and Catholic Christianity

These Exam Practice Tips will give you helpful hints about how to do better in the exam or how to improve your revision.

Tick one of these boxes depending on how confident you feel with the questions in each topic. This should help show you where you need to focus your revision.

This question is only for students studying Catholic Christianity.

Some questions (or whole pages) in the Christianity and Catholic Christianity section will have a note like this, to let you know who the questions are suitable for — some are only for students studying Catholic Christianity, and some are only for students studying Christianity. Make sure you pay attention to these notes and don't answer questions you don't need to.

Getting Started

Exam Breakdown

This book is packed full of exam practice to help you get ready for your exams and figure out what you should be revising. Answer questions on the topics you've studied and see how well you do. Then, if there are any topics you've struggled with, go back and revise them again. But first, here's a quick breakdown of the exams you'll have to do and what they'll be like.

You'll have to do Two Exams

1) For GCSE AQA A Religious Studies, you'll have to sit two exams — one on the two religions you've studied and one on the themes you've studied.

2) If you've done the textual studies on St Mark's Gospel (Themes G and H), you'll answer questions on Christianity or Catholic Christianity in Paper 1, as well as questions on one other religion. In Paper 2, you'll answer questions on the two religious, philosophical and ethical themes you've covered (Themes A-F), and then answer the questions on the two themes on St Mark's Gospel (Themes G and H).

3) If you haven't done the textual studies on St Mark's Gospel, you'll answer questions on the two religions you've studied for Paper 1. In Paper 2, you'll answer questions on the four themes you've studied.

4) Here's a little bit more info on exactly what each exam will be like.

Paper 1: Religious Beliefs

1) Paper 1 is on the beliefs, teachings and practices of religions.
2) You'll be given two booklets, one for each of the two religions you've studied.
3) There will be two questions in each booklet — one on 'beliefs' and one on 'practices'.
4) Each question will have five parts — worth 1, 2, 4, 5 and 12 marks each.
5) You should aim to spend about 25 minutes on each question.
6) Both 12 mark question parts on 'beliefs' will also have an extra 3 marks available for spelling, punctuation and grammar.
7) 1 hour 45 minutes | 102 marks in total | 50% of your final mark

Paper 2: Thematic Studies

1) Paper 2 is on thematic studies.
2) You'll be given one booklet containing six or eight questions — eight questions if you've done the textual studies on St Mark's Gospel, six questions otherwise.
3) You should answer four of the questions on the four themes you've studied.
4) Each question will have five parts — worth 1, 2, 4, 5 and 12 marks each.
5) You should aim to spend about 25 minutes on each question.
6) For each 12 mark question part, you'll be given a mark out of 3 for spelling, punctuation and grammar — but only the best mark out of all of these will be counted towards your total.
7) 1 hour 45 minutes | 99 marks in total | 50% of your final mark

Only Answer Questions on Topics You've Studied

1) You'll need to answer four questions on each paper you sit — that's two questions on each religion you've studied and one question on every theme you've studied.

2) For Paper 2, make sure you know what themes you studied and answer those questions — and only those. Don't waste time writing an answer for a topic you don't know about.

3) For Paper 1, this book contains practice questions on Christianity and Catholic Christianity and Islam. Remember, you can't sit your exam on Christianity and Catholic Christianity — it's one or the other.

4) For Paper 2, this book contains practice questions on all eight themes.

If you've studied more than four themes, you still only need to answer four questions.

Getting Started

Beliefs, Teachings and Practices — Christianity and Catholic Christianity

The Nature of God

1   Which of the following is **not** a belief about the Trinity?
    Put a tick (✓) in the correct box.

    A   Each person of the Trinity has a different role.   ☐

    B   The Father is the most important person of the Trinity.   ☐

    C   The Holy Spirit guides Christians and the Church itself.   ☐

    D   Jesus is God in human form.   ☐

    [1 mark]

2   Which of the following means to be present in the physical world,
    or to interact with humanity? Put a tick (✓) in the correct box.

    A   Omnipotent   ☐

    B   Transcendent   ☐

    C   Benevolent   ☐

    D   Immanent   ☐

    [1 mark]

3   Give the names of two Christian denominations.

    1) ....

    ....

    2) ....

    ....
    [2 marks]

4   'A belief in the Trinity is the most important Christian belief.'   (SPaG MARKS)

    Evaluate this statement. Your answer should include the following:
    • examples from Christian teachings
    • arguments that support the statement
    • arguments that disagree with the statement
    • a conclusion.

    Write your answer on a separate sheet of paper.

    [12 marks]

Exam Tip

When it comes to 2 mark questions, your answers don't have to be really long at all. You don't even have to write in full sentences if you don't think you need to — just a word or a phrase could be enough to pick up the marks that you're looking for. Just make sure you write enough to clearly answer the question.

Score: /16

Creation

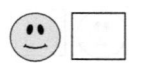

1 Which of the following occurred during the creation story?
Put a tick (✓) in the correct box.

    A   The moon and the oceans were created on the same day. ☐

    B   People were created on the third day. ☐

    C   Land animals were created on the same day as people. ☐

    D   The sun was created on the first day. ☐

[1 mark]

2 Explain two ways in which beliefs about the creation of humans influence Christians today.

....

....

....

....

....

[4 marks]

3 Explain two ways in which the creation story influences
the way Christians understand God and the universe.
Your answer should refer to specific Christian teachings or sacred texts.

....

....

....

....

....

....

[5 marks]

Score: ☐
10

Beliefs, Teachings and Practices — Christianity and Catholic Christianity

Evil and Suffering

If you're studying Catholic Christianity, you don't need to answer the questions on this page.

1 Which of the following is **not** a Christian belief about evil? Put a tick (✓) in the correct box.

    A   There are two types of evil in the world. ☐

    B   Natural evil includes things like earthquakes and floods. ☐

    C   Moral evil comes from human beings. ☐

    D   Evil is always more powerful than good. ☐

[1 mark]

2 Which of the following is the belief that all humans are born with the potential to cause suffering and do wrong? Put a tick (✓) in the correct box.

    A   The Fall ☐

    B   Original sin ☐

    C   Moral evil ☐

    D   Salvation ☐

[1 mark]

3 Give two Christian beliefs about evil found in the story of Adam and Eve.

1) ....

....

2) ....

....

[2 marks]

4 'The existence of evil proves that the Christian God does not exist.'

(SPaG MARKS)

Evaluate this statement. Your answer should include the following:
- examples from Christian teachings
- arguments that support the statement
- arguments that disagree with the statement
- a conclusion.

Write your answer on a separate sheet of paper.

[12 marks]

Score: ☐ / 16

Beliefs, Teachings and Practices — Christianity and Catholic Christianity

The Afterlife

1 Which of the following is the place where people are purified after death?
Put a tick (✓) in the correct box.

This question is only for students studying Catholic Christianity.

- **A** Heaven ☐
- **B** Purgatory ☐
- **C** Immortality ☐
- **D** Hell ☐

[1 mark]

2 Explain two ways in which the idea of judgement influences Christians today.

....
....
....
....
....

[4 marks]

3 Explain two Christian teachings on heaven.
Your answer should refer to specific Christian teachings or sacred texts.

....
....
....
....
....
....

[5 marks]

Score: ☐
10

Beliefs, Teachings and Practices — Christianity and Catholic Christianity

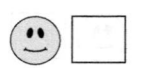

Jesus Christ and Salvation

1 Which of the following is the meaning of the term 'incarnation'?
Put a tick (✓) in the correct box.

- A God becoming human ☐
- B Jesus being crowned king ☐
- C Jesus going up to heaven ☐
- D Jesus coming back to life ☐

[1 mark]

2 Which of the following means love from God which mankind doesn't deserve?
Put a tick (✓) in the correct box.

- A Salvation ☐
- B Redemption ☐
- C Grace ☐
- D Reconciliation ☐

[1 mark]

3 Give two Christian beliefs about Jesus's ascension.

1) ....

....

2) ....

....

[2 marks]

4 Explain two ways in which beliefs about incarnation influence Christians.

....

....

....

....

....

[4 marks]

Beliefs, Teachings and Practices — Christianity and Catholic Christianity

5 Give two Christian beliefs about redemption.

1) ....

....

2) ....

....

[2 marks]

6 Explain two Christian teachings about resurrection.
Your answer should refer to specific Christian teachings or sacred texts.

....

....

....

....

....

....

....

[5 marks]

7 'Jesus's death on the cross is more important to Christians than his resurrection.'

Evaluate this statement. Your answer should include the following:
- examples from Christian teachings
- arguments that support the statement
- arguments that disagree with the statement
- a conclusion.

Write your answer on a separate sheet of paper.

(SPaG MARKS)

[12 marks]

Exam Tip

You'll answer a 12 mark question on 'beliefs' for each of the two religions you've studied. Each of these questions has 3 marks available for SPaG, so take care with your writing in these. If you get your punctuation and grammar right, and spell everything correctly, you'll have 6 marks in the bag...

Score ☐ / 27

Beliefs, Teachings and Practices — Christianity and Catholic Christianity

Worship and Prayer

1 Which of the following is a type of prayer asking God for something?
Put a tick (✓) in the correct box.

    A   Adoration ☐

    B   Supplication ☐

    C   Thanksgiving ☐

    D   Confession ☐

[1 mark]

2 Which of the following is **not** regularly included in a weekly church service?
Put a tick (✓) in the correct box.

    A   Bible readings ☐

    B   Prayers ☐

    C   A baptism ☐

    D   A sermon ☐

[1 mark]

3 Give two reasons why Catholics pray with a rosary.

This question is only for students studying Catholic Christianity.

1) ....

....

2) ....

....

[2 marks]

4 Explain two contrasting views on how close Christians are to God during public and private worship.

....

....

....

....

....

[4 marks]

Beliefs, Teachings and Practices — Christianity and Catholic Christianity

5 Which of the following is a description of the 'Stations of the Cross'?
Put a tick (✓) in the correct box.

This question is only for students studying Catholic Christianity.

    A   Pictures of Jesus's suffering ☐

    B   A necklace of beads ☐

    C   Locations on a pilgrimage ☐

    D   The place where Jesus was crucified ☐

[1 mark]

6 Explain two ways in which the Lord's Prayer is important to Christians.
Your answer should refer to specific Christian teachings or sacred texts.

....

....

....

....

....

....

....

[5 marks]

7 'Informal prayer is more important to Christians than formal prayer.'

Evaluate this statement. Your answer should include the following:
- examples from Christian teachings
- arguments that support the statement
- arguments that disagree with the statement
- a conclusion.

Write your answer on a separate sheet of paper.

[12 marks]

Exam Tip

For 12 mark questions, it's good to jot down a quick plan to get your ideas down before diving in — it'll be easier for you to give a logical, well-argued answer. Think of a few arguments that support the statement, and a few that don't, to help create a balanced discussion. Just put a line through your plan when you're finished.

Score ☐ / 26

Beliefs, Teachings and Practices — Christianity and Catholic Christianity

The Sacraments

1 Which of the following is a ceremony where Christians who were baptised as babies affirm their faith? Put a tick (✓) in the correct box.

- A   Confirmation ☐
- B   Contrition ☐
- C   Marriage ☐
- D   Holy orders ☐

[1 mark]

2 Which of the following is the event which Christians re-enact with the Eucharist (Holy Communion)? Put a tick (✓) in the correct box.

- A   The feeding of the five thousand ☐
- B   The Last Supper ☐
- C   The Sermon on the Mount ☐
- D   Jesus's ascension into heaven ☐

[1 mark]

3 Give two sacraments that Protestant Christians believe they should perform.

1) ....

....

2) ....

....

[2 marks]

4 Explain two contrasting views about infant baptism.

....

....

....

....

....

....

[4 marks]

Beliefs, Teachings and Practices — Christianity and Catholic Christianity

5 Which of the following is **not** part of the sacrament of reconciliation? Put a tick (✓) in the correct box.

This question is only for students studying Catholic Christianity.

- A   Confession ☐
- B   Penance ☐
- C   Absolution ☐
- D   Anointing ☐

[1 mark]

6 Explain two reasons why Catholic Christians perform the sacrament of anointing the sick. Your answer should refer to specific Christian teachings or sacred texts.

This question is only for students studying Catholic Christianity.

....

....

....

....

....

....

[5 marks]

7 'The presence of the actual body and blood of Christ is what makes the Eucharist (Holy Communion) important.'

Evaluate this statement. Your answer should include the following:
- examples from Christian teachings
- arguments that support the statement
- arguments that disagree with the statement
- a conclusion.

Write your answer on a separate sheet of paper.

[12 marks]

> **Exam Tip**
> For 5 mark questions, you need to refer to specific religious teachings or sacred texts. Always say where the teaching you quote or describe comes from — for Christian beliefs and practices, this could be the Bible, the Catechism of the Catholic Church, Articles of the Church of England, or any other official Church teaching.

Score ☐ / 26

Beliefs, Teachings and Practices — Christianity and Catholic Christianity

Pilgrimage

1 Which of the following is an event in the Bible which some Christians consider to be an example of pilgrimage? Put a tick (✓) in the correct box.

- A   Jesus and his parents' journey to Jerusalem ☐
- B   Jesus's temptation in the desert ☐
- C   Mary and Joseph's journey to Bethlehem ☐
- D   Jesus walking to the place where he was crucified ☐

[1 mark]

2 Which of the following is **not** a major reason why Christians might go on a pilgrimage? Put a tick (✓) in the correct box.

- A   To preach the Gospel ☐
- B   To ask for healing ☐
- C   To escape everyday life ☐
- D   To find a deeper connection with God ☐

[1 mark]

3 Give two examples of popular destinations for Christian pilgrims.

1) ....

....

2) ....

....

[2 marks]

4 'Pilgrimage is not important for modern Christians.'

Evaluate this statement. Your answer should include the following:
- examples from Christian teachings
- arguments that support the statement
- arguments that disagree with the statement
- a conclusion.

Write your answer on a separate sheet of paper.

[12 marks]

Score: ☐ / 16

Beliefs, Teachings and Practices — Christianity and Catholic Christianity

Christmas and Easter

If you're studying Catholic Christianity, you don't need to answer the questions on this page.

1   Which of the following is the first day of Lent?
    Put a tick (✓) in the correct box.

    A   Easter Sunday   ☐
    B   Shrove Tuesday ☐
    C   Ash Wednesday   ☐
    D   Good Friday   ☐

[1 mark]

2   Explain two contrasting Christian views on the importance of Christmas.

    ....
    ....
    ....
    ....
    ....

[4 marks]

3   Explain two ways in which Christians mark the approach and celebration of Easter.
    Your answer should refer to specific Christian teachings or sacred texts.

    ....
    ....
    ....
    ....
    ....
    ....

[5 marks]

Score: ☐

10

Beliefs, Teachings and Practices — Christianity and Catholic Christianity

The Work of the Church

1 Which of the following is an international Christian organisation?
Put a tick (✓) in the correct box.

    A   WaterAid ☐

    B   UNICEF ☐

    C   CAFOD ☐

    D   Plan UK ☐

[1 mark]

2 Which of the following is **not** a reason why Christians believe it is important to give to charity?
Put a tick (✓) in the correct box.

    A   The Bible teaches that all humans beings are equal and have dignity. ☐

    B   Jesus cared for the poor. ☐

    C   Jesus taught that Christians should love their neighbours. ☐

    D   It is difficult for the poor to enter the kingdom of God. ☐

[1 mark]

3 Give two Christian charities that work in the UK.

1) ....

....

2) ....

....

[2 marks]

4 Explain two contrasting views on the importance of evangelism.

....

....

....

....

....

....

[4 marks]

Beliefs, Teachings and Practices — Christianity and Catholic Christianity

5 Which of the following is a description of what a missionary does?
Put a tick (✓) in the correct box.

    A   Spreads the word of God abroad ☐

    B   Spreads the word of God in their local community ☐

    C   Gives money to local charities ☐

    D   Gives money to international charities ☐

[1 mark]

6 Explain two reasons why Christian organisations work to promote reconciliation. Your answer should refer to specific Christian teachings or sacred texts.

....

....

....

....

....

....

[5 marks]

7 'The most important role of Christian churches is to build a community of Christians in their local area.'

Evaluate this statement. Your answer should include the following:
- examples from Christian teachings
- arguments that support the statement
- arguments that disagree with the statement
- a conclusion.

Write your answer on a separate sheet of paper.

[12 marks]

Exam Tip

If you're having trouble answering some questions, go back to your study notes and/or revision guide and refresh your memory on the topics you're struggling with. Then, once you're more comfortable with the topic, try covering your notes so you can't see them and have another bash at answering the questions.

Score ☐ / 26

Beliefs, Teachings and Practices — Christianity and Catholic Christianity

Key Beliefs in Islam

1 Which of the following means that God is good?
Put a tick (✓) in the correct box.

- A Just ☐
- B Transcendent ☐
- C Immanent ☐
- D Beneficent ☐

[1 mark]

2 Which of the following is the belief in angels?
Put a tick (✓) in the correct box.

- A al-Qadr ☐
- B Nubuwwah ☐
- C Sunni ☐
- D Malaikah ☐

[1 mark]

3 Give two articles of faith in Sunni Islam.

1) ....

....

2) ....

....

[2 marks]

4 Explain two ways in which belief in Tawhid might influence Muslims today.

....

....

....

....

....

[4 marks]

5 Which of the following is the Islamic term for belief in more than one god?
Put a tick (✓) in the correct box.

    A   Ma'ad ☐

    B   Tawhid ☐

    C   Shirk ☐

    D   Hadith ☐

[1 mark]

6 Explain two Muslim beliefs about the nature of God.
Your answer should refer to specific Muslim teachings or sacred texts.

....

....

....

....

....

....

....

[5 marks]

7 'Sunni and Shi'a Muslims have very different perspectives on Islam.'

(SPaG MARKS)

Evaluate this statement. Your answer should include the following:
- examples from Muslim teachings
- arguments that support the statement
- arguments that disagree with the statement
- a conclusion.

Write your answer on a separate sheet of paper.

[12 marks]

Exam Tip

In the exam, you don't need to write loads and loads. What you need to do is show that you have a lot of knowledge and understanding of the topics you're writing about, so that you demonstrate to the examiner that you know your stuff. So try and get to the point quickly and show off everything you've learned.

Score ☐ / 26

Beliefs, Teachings and Practices — Islam

Authority

1 Which of the following do Muslims believe was a prophet?
Put a tick (✓) in the correct box.

    A   Jibril   ☐

    B   Mika'il   ☐

    C   Ibrahim   ☐

    D   Iblis   ☐

[1 mark]

2 Which of the following means 'leadership' or 'authority of the imams' to Shi'a Muslims?
Put a tick (✓) in the correct box.

    A   Imamate   ☐

    B   Tawhid   ☐

    C   Adalat   ☐

    D   Nubuwwah   ☐

[1 mark]

3 Give two beliefs about the imams in Shi'a Islam.

1) ....

....

2) ....

....

[2 marks]

4 Explain two ways in which belief about the Qur'an may influence Muslims today.

....

....

....

....

....

[4 marks]

Beliefs, Teachings and Practices — Islam

5 Which of the following means a chapter of the Qur'an?
Put a tick (✓) in the correct box.

A   Ayah   ☐

B   Hadith   ☐

C   Sunnah   ☐

D   Surah   ☐

[1 mark]

6 Explain two Muslim beliefs about holy books other than the Qur'an.
Your answer should refer to specific Muslim teachings or sacred texts.

....

....

....

....

....

....

[5 marks]

7 'Muhammad's main role was to communicate Allah's message in the Qur'an.'

Evaluate this statement. Your answer should include the following:
- examples from Muslim teachings
- arguments that support the statement
- arguments that disagree with the statement
- a conclusion.

Write your answer on a separate sheet of paper.

[12 marks]

Exam Tip
You need to do lots of things right to get full marks on a 12 mark question. The question will tell you all the things you need to cover — and it'll say if there are marks for spelling, punctuation and grammar. As you're writing your answer, make sure you've covered all the bullet points — check it at the end to make sure of this.

Score ☐ / 26

Beliefs, Teachings and Practices — Islam

Life After Death

1 Which of the following is the belief in life after death?
Put a tick (✓) in the correct box.

    A   Nubuwwah ☐

    B   al-Akhirah ☐

    C   Imamate ☐

    D   Tawhid ☐

[1 mark]

2 Which of the following gives the meaning of 'jannah'?
Put a tick (✓) in the correct box.

    A   Angel of death ☐

    B   Resurrection ☐

    C   Paradise ☐

    D   Hell ☐

[1 mark]

3 Give two Muslim beliefs about what will happen on the Day of Judgement.

    1) ....

    ....

    2) ....

    ....

[2 marks]

4 'It is impossible to believe in both predestination and free will.'   *(SPaG MARKS)*

Evaluate this statement. Your answer should include the following:
- examples from Muslim teachings
- arguments that support the statement
- arguments that disagree with the statement
- a conclusion.

Write your answer on a separate sheet of paper.

[12 marks]

Exam Tip

To get top marks in a 12 mark question, you need to use a lot of relevant, specialist terms, so don't forget to use them in your answers when you can. It's important to make sure you know Islam-specific key words and phrases for each topic, as well as how to spell them for those spelling, punctuation and grammar marks.

Score   16

Beliefs, Teachings and Practices — Islam

Worship

1 Which of the following is the ritual washing before prayer?
Put a tick (✓) in the correct box.

    A   Zakah ☐

    B   Hajj ☐

    C   Rak'ah ☐

    D   Wudu ☐

[1 mark]

2 Explain two contrasting ways in which Salah is performed.

....

....

....

....

....

....

[4 marks]

3 Explain two reasons why Shahadah is important to Muslims.
Your answer should refer to specific Muslim religious teachings or sacred texts.

....

....

....

....

....

....

[5 marks]

Score: ☐
10

Beliefs, Teachings and Practices — Islam

Duties

1 Which of the following means the simple white clothing worn on Hajj?
Put a tick (✓) in the correct box.

- A　Ka'aba ☐
- B　Mina ☐
- C　Sawm ☐
- D　Ihram ☐

[1 mark]

2 Which of the following is the name given to the celebration of the 'Night of Power', the commemoration of Muhammad first receiving the Qur'an? Put a tick (✓) in the correct box.

- A　Laylat al-Qadr ☐
- B　Zakah ☐
- C　Ashura ☐
- D　Id-ul-Adha ☐

[1 mark]

3 Give two places that Muslims visit on the hajj journey.

1) ....

....

2) ....

....

[2 marks]

4 Explain two contrasting understandings of charity.

....

....

....

....

....

....

[4 marks]

Beliefs, Teachings and Practices — Islam

5 Which of the following gives the meaning of the term 'jihad'?
Put a tick (✓) in the correct box.

- A Journey ☐
- B Fasting ☐
- C Struggle ☐
- D Charity ☐

[1 mark]

6 Explain two ways in which sawm is important to Muslims.
Your answer should refer to specific Muslim teachings or sacred texts.

....

....

....

....

....

....

[5 marks]

7 'Jihad should be the main duty in a Muslim's life.'

Evaluate this statement. Your answer should include the following:
- examples from Muslim teachings
- arguments that support the statement
- arguments that disagree with the statement
- a conclusion.

Write your answer on a separate sheet of paper.

[12 marks]

Exam Tip

You need to give evidence in your answers for 5 mark questions — for the Islam paper, this could come from the Qur'an, the Hadith or other relevant texts. Jot down any quotes that could be useful, and go over them as you revise. In the exam, you can quote them or paraphrase what they say — it'll get you an extra mark.

Festivals

1 Which of the following is a prophet celebrated by Muslims during Id-ul-Adha?
Put a tick (✓) in the correct box.

    A   Isa ☐

    B   Muhammad ☐

    C   Musa ☐

    D   Ibrahim ☐

[1 mark]

2 Explain two contrasting ways of marking the festival of Ashura.

....

....

....

....

....

....

[4 marks]

3 Explain two reasons why Id-ul-Fitr is important to Muslims.
Your answer should refer to specific Muslim teachings or sacred texts.

....

....

....

....

....

....

....

[5 marks]

Score: ☐ / 10

Sexuality and Sexual Relationships

1 Which of the following is the term for having multiple sexual partners?
Put a tick (✓) in the correct box.

- A Monogamy ☐
- B Promiscuity ☐
- C Heterosexuality ☐
- D Celibacy ☐

[1 mark]

2 Explain two similar religious beliefs in British society today about homosexuality.
You must refer to the main religious tradition in the UK and at least one other religious viewpoint.

....

....

....

....

....

[4 marks]

3 Explain two religious beliefs about contraception.
Your answer should refer to specific religious teachings or sacred texts.

....

....

....

....

....

[5 marks]

Score: ☐ / 10

Marriage and Divorce

1 Which of the following describes the legal ending of a marriage?
Put a tick (✓) in the correct box.

    A   Polygamy ☐

    B   Divorce ☐

    C   Remarriage ☐

    D   Promiscuity ☐

[1 mark]

2 Give two religious beliefs about same-sex marriage.

1) ....

....

2) ....

....

[2 marks]

3 Give two religious beliefs about divorce.

1) ....

....

2) ....

....

[2 marks]

4 Explain two contrasting beliefs regarding cohabitation.
You must refer to the views of at least one religious group.

....

....

....

....

....

[4 marks]

Theme A — Relationships and Families

5 Which of the following is the term for being unfaithful to your marriage partner?
Put a tick (✓) in the correct box.

    A   Cohabitation ☐

    B   Divorce ☐

    C   Adultery ☐

    D   Annulment ☐

[1 mark]

6 Explain two religious beliefs about the purpose of marriage.
Your answer should refer to specific religious teachings or sacred texts.

....

....

....

....

....

....

....

[5 marks]

7 'Divorced people should not be allowed to remarry.'

(SPaG MARKS)

Evaluate this statement. Your answer should include the following:
- religious arguments that support the statement
- religious arguments that disagree with the statement
- a conclusion.

You can also include non-religious points of view in your answer.

Write your answer on a separate sheet of paper.

[12 marks]

Exam Tip

There are up to 3 extra marks for spelling, punctuation and grammar (SPaG) on all 12 mark questions in the 'Themes' part of the exam. They will only be counted for one of the questions — the one with the best SPaG score will be used. Read through your 12 mark answers to check for SPaG errors that might have slipped in.

Score ☐ / 27

Theme A — Relationships and Families

Families

1 Which of the following terms describes a family where a couple live together with their children?
Put a tick (✓) in the correct box.

- **A** Nuclear ☐
- **B** Extended ☐
- **C** Beanpole ☐
- **D** Single-parent ☐

[1 mark]

2 Explain two contrasting beliefs about same-sex parenting.
You must refer to the views of at least one religious group.

....

....

....

....

....

....

[4 marks]

3 Explain two religious beliefs about educating children in a religious family.
Your answer should refer to specific religious teachings or sacred texts.

....

....

....

....

....

....

....

[5 marks]

Score: ☐ / 10

Gender Equality

1 Which of the following terms implies that men and women might not be viewed as equals in British society? Put a tick (✓) in the correct box.

- A Transgender ☐
- B Gender inequality ☐
- C Liturgy ☐
- D Harassment ☐

[1 mark]

2 Which of the following allows parents to share the time they can take off work following the birth of a baby? Put a tick (✓) in the correct box.

- A Maternity leave ☐
- B Annual leave ☐
- C Shared parental leave ☐
- D Paternity leave ☐

[1 mark]

3 Give two religious beliefs about gender discrimination.

1) ....

....

2) ....

....

[2 marks]

4 'Men and women are equal and should have equal status within the family.'

(SPaG MARKS)

Evaluate this statement. Your answer should include the following:
- religious arguments that support the statement
- religious arguments that disagree with the statement
- a conclusion.

You can also include non-religious points of view in your answer.

Write your answer on a separate sheet of paper.

[12 marks]

Exam Tip

Don't forget to write a conclusion when you're answering a 12 mark question — you won't be able to get top marks without one. When you're writing your conclusion, you should sum up what you've discussed in your answer, and clearly say whether you agree or disagree with the statement that the question asked you about.

Score ☐ / 16

Theme A — Relationships and Families

Theme B — Religion and Life

The Universe and the Environment

1 Which of the following is a scientific theory about the origins of the universe?
Put a tick (✓) in the correct box.

- **A** The Big Bang theory ☐
- **B** The theory of gravity ☐
- **C** Genesis ☐
- **D** The story of creation ☐

[1 mark]

2 Which of the following is the idea that humans have power over nature?
Put a tick (✓) in the correct box.

- **A** Dominion ☐
- **B** Stewardship ☐
- **C** Creation ☐
- **D** Humanism ☐

[1 mark]

3 Give two religious beliefs about the creation of the universe.

1) ....

....

2) ....

....

[2 marks]

4 Explain two similar religious beliefs about the environment.
You must refer to the views of at least one religious group.

....

....

....

....

....

[4 marks]

Theme B — Religion and Life

5 Which of the following is an argument used to justify eating meat?
Put a tick (✓) in the correct box.

    A   Animals bred for meat often suffer. ☐

    B   Humans don't need meat to survive. ☑

    C   Eating meat is good for the environment. ☐

    D   Only human life is sacred. ☐

[1 mark]

6 Explain two religious beliefs about the origins of human life.
Your answer should refer to specific religious teachings or sacred texts.

....

....

....

....

....

....

[5 marks]

7 'Performing experiments on animals is always wrong.'

(SPaG MARKS)

Evaluate this statement. Your answer should include the following:
- religious arguments that support the statement
- religious arguments that disagree with the statement
- a conclusion.

You can also include non-religious points of view in your answer.

Write your answer on a separate sheet of paper.

[12 marks]

Exam Tip

If you're asked to compare two viewpoints for 4 mark questions, you can give two different views from the same religion, as in "some Christians believe..." and "other Christians believe...". Or you can give views from two different religions. Just make sure the views are similar or contrasting, depending on what's asked for.

Score ☐ / 26

Theme B — Religion and Life

Abortion and Euthanasia

1 Which of the following is the meaning of the word 'abortion'?
Put a tick (✓) in the correct box.

    A   When a pregnancy is deliberately ended without the birth of a living child. ☐

    B   Helping someone die to relieve their suffering. ☐

    C   When a foetus cannot survive after birth so it is removed from the womb. ☐

    D   Helping someone die because they have a terminal illness. ☐

[1 mark]

2 Which of the following is a common argument for euthanasia?
Put a tick (✓) in the correct box.

    A   Life is sacred so humans should not end life on purpose. ☐

    B   God created each person so everyone's life belongs to God. ☐

    C   The patient is not terminally ill. ☐

    D   The patient's quality of life is so bad that death is more compassionate. ☐

[1 mark]

3 Give two situations when abortion is allowed according to UK law.

1) ....

....

2) ....

....

[2 marks]

4 Explain two contrasting beliefs in British society today about the sanctity of life.
You must refer to the main religious tradition in the UK and at least one other religious viewpoint.

....

....

....

....

....

[4 marks]

5 Which of the following is a country where euthanasia is legal?
Put a tick (✓) in the correct box.

    A   UK   ☐

    B   Belgium   ☐

    C   Russia   ☐

    D   France   ☐

[1 mark]

6 Explain two religious beliefs about euthanasia.
Your answer should refer to specific religious teachings or sacred texts.

....

....

....

....

....

....

[5 marks]

7 'Abortion is acceptable in certain circumstances.'

    (SPaG MARKS)

Evaluate this statement. Your answer should include the following:
- religious arguments that support the statement
- religious arguments that disagree with the statement
- a conclusion.

You can also include non-religious points of view in your answer.

Write your answer on a separate sheet of paper.

[12 marks]

Exam Tip

Abortion and euthanasia are very difficult issues, and there are many different beliefs about them, even within the same religion. Many people believe that the circumstances matter in cases of abortion and euthanasia — these are really complex issues, so make sure you feel confident writing about different perspectives on them.

Score: / 26

Theme B — Religion and Life

The Afterlife

1 Which of the following is **not** an argument for the existence of the afterlife?
Put a tick (✓) in the correct box.

    A   Young children sometimes describe memories of past lives. ☐

    B   Some people claim to have seen the ghost of people who have died. ☐

    C   Believing in the afterlife is a comfort to people when someone dies. ☐

    D   Many sacred texts describe an afterlife. ☐

[1 mark]

2 Which of the following is the word for being reborn after death into a new body?
Put a tick (✓) in the correct box.

    A   Judgement ☐

    B   Purgatory ☐

    C   Reincarnation ☐

    D   Resurrection ☐

[1 mark]

3 Give two arguments against the existence of an afterlife.

1) ....

....

2) ....

....

[2 marks]

4 'The afterlife is more important than life on Earth.'

(SPaG MARKS)

Evaluate this statement. Your answer should include the following:
- religious arguments that support the statement
- religious arguments that disagree with the statement
- a conclusion.

You can also include non-religious points of view in your answer.

Write your answer on a separate sheet of paper.

[12 marks]

Score: ☐ / 16

Theme B — Religion and Life

Theme C — The Existence of God and Revelation

Design and Causation

1 Which of the following is the scientist who is famous for developing the theory of evolution? Put a tick (✓) in the correct box.

- A Marie Curie ☐
- B Charles Darwin ☐
- C Al-Ghazali ☐
- D Thomas Aquinas ☐

[1 mark]

2 Which of the following did William Paley write about as part of his Design argument? Put a tick (✓) in the correct box.

- A A watch ☐
- B A camera ☐
- C The human ear ☐
- D The human heart ☐

[1 mark]

3 Give two strengths of the Design argument.

1) ....
....

2) ....
....

[2 marks]

4 'The First Cause argument is proof that God exists.'

(SPaG MARKS)

Evaluate this statement. Your answer should include the following:
- religious arguments that support the statement
- religious arguments that disagree with the statement
- a conclusion.

You can also include non-religious points of view in your answer.

Write your answer on a separate sheet of paper.

[12 marks]

Exam Tip

The Design and First Cause arguments can be really tricky, so make sure you've got your head around them before the exam. Try covering your notes and jotting down a quick summary of both arguments, then check to see how much of them you have remembered. Use a different colour pen to add in the points you missed.

Score ☐ / 16

Miracles and Revelation

1 Which of the following is the meaning of the word 'transcendent'?
Put a tick (✓) in the correct box.

    A   All-powerful ☐

    B   Part of the physical world ☐

    C   Able to travel anywhere at any time ☐

    D   Separate from the world ☐

[1 mark]

2 Which of the following is a form of special revelation?
Put a tick (✓) in the correct box.

    A   Nature ☐

    B   Morality ☐

    C   Visions ☐

    D   Philosophy ☐

[1 mark]

3 Give two examples of miracles found in major religious texts.

1) ....

....

2) ....

....

[2 marks]

4 Give two reasons why people might not believe that religious experiences prove God's existence.

1) ....

....

2) ....

....

[2 marks]

5 Which of the following is **not** a reason why religious scriptures are viewed as important? Put a tick (✓) in the correct box.

- A They were written centuries ago ☐
- B They reveal God's will ☐
- C They show us God's nature ☐
- D They come directly from God or were inspired by him ☐

[1 mark]

6 Explain two religious beliefs about how nature shows the existence of God. Your answer should refer to specific religious teachings or sacred texts.

....
....
....
....
....
....
....

[5 marks]

7 Explain two contrasting beliefs in British society today about general revelation. You must refer to the main religious tradition in the UK and non-religious viewpoints.

....
....
....
....
....
....

[4 marks]

8 Explain two religious beliefs about revelation in scripture.
Your answer should refer to specific religious teachings or sacred texts.

....

....

....

....

....

....

[5 marks]

9 Explain two similar religious beliefs about miracles.

....

....

....

....

....

[4 marks]

10 'Visions prove that God exists.'

(SPaG MARKS)

Evaluate this statement. Your answer should include the following:
- religious arguments that support the statement
- religious arguments that disagree with the statement
- a conclusion.

You can also include non-religious points of view in your answer.

Write your answer on a separate sheet of paper.

[12 marks]

Exam Tip

In Theme C you must use arguments based on the religions you've studied, but you can also use non-religious arguments. But remember — if the question asks about views in British society today or asks you to refer to the main religious tradition in the UK, then you must talk about Christianity as well as other viewpoints.

Score ☐ / 37

Theme C — The Existence of God and Revelation

Arguments Against the Existence of God

1 Which of the following is the name for someone who does not believe in God? Put a tick (✓) in the correct box.

- A   Atheist ☐
- B   Agnostic ☐
- C   Theist ☐
- D   Monotheist ☐

[1 mark]

2 Which of the following is a reason why non-religious people might dismiss miracles as proof of God's existence? Put a tick (✓) in the correct box.

- A   There isn't enough scientific evidence that they happened. ☐
- B   Miracles are only ever witnessed by one person. ☐
- C   It is completely impossible for reports of these things to survive. ☐
- D   There aren't enough examples of miracles to offer proof. ☐

[1 mark]

3 Give two scientific arguments against the existence of God.

1) ....

....

2) ....

....

[2 marks]

4 Explain two contrasting beliefs about why evil and suffering exist in the world. You must refer to the views of at least one religious group.

....

....

....

....

[4 marks]

Score: ☐ / 8

Theme C — The Existence of God and Revelation

Theme D — Religion, Peace and Conflict

Peace and Conflict

1 Which of the following means deliberately causing harm or injury while campaigning for a cause? Put a tick (✓) in the correct box.

- **A** Tribalism ☐
- **B** Discrimination ☐
- **C** Violent protest ☐
- **D** Conversion ☐

[1 mark]

2 Which of the following describes no longer feeling angry because of something another person has done? Put a tick (✓) in the correct box.

- **A** Repentance ☐
- **B** Pacifism ☐
- **C** Retaliation ☐
- **D** Forgiveness ☐

[1 mark]

3 Give two criteria for a just war.

1) ....

....

2) ....

....

[2 marks]

4 Explain two similar religious beliefs about terrorism.
You must refer to the views of at least one religious group.

....

....

....

....

....

....

[4 marks]

5 Which of the following means a conflict fought by those who believe they are supported by God? Put a tick (✓) in the correct box.

    A   Just War ☐

    B   Holy War ☐

    C   Self-defence ☐

    D   Terrorism ☐

[1 mark]

6 Explain two religious beliefs about reconciliation.
Your answer should refer to specific religious teachings or sacred texts.

....

....

....

....

....

....

[5 marks]

7 'Religion should never be used to justify violence.'

(SPaG MARKS)

Evaluate this statement. Your answer should include the following:
- religious arguments that support the statement
- religious arguments that disagree with the statement
- a conclusion.

You can also include non-religious points of view in your answer.

Write your answer on a separate sheet of paper.

[12 marks]

Exam Tip

Try to leave yourself enough time at the end of the exam to check over your answers — especially for the 12 mark question. Read through your answer, checking all the spelling, punctuation and grammar are correct (remember, there are 3 extra marks for this) — and make sure everything you've written is relevant.

Score ☐ / 26

Theme D — Religion, Peace and Conflict

Weapons of Mass Destruction

1   Which of the following is a term used to describe weapons which cause harm to civilians and soldiers alike? Put a tick (✓) in the correct box.

    A   Non-lethal   ☐

    B   Reconciliation   ☐

    C   Retribution   ☐

    D   Indiscriminate   ☐

[1 mark]

2   Explain two contrasting beliefs in British society today about the possession of nuclear weapons. You must refer to the main religious tradition in the UK and at least one other religious viewpoint.

....

....

....

....

....

[4 marks]

3   Explain two religious beliefs about the use of weapons of mass destruction. Your answer should refer to specific religious teachings or sacred texts.

....

....

....

....

....

....

[5 marks]

Score: ☐ / 10

Peacemaking

1 Which of the following is **not** an element of peacemaking?
Put a tick (✓) in the correct box.

- A   Justice ☐
- B   Retaliation ☐
- C   Forgiveness ☐
- D   Reconciliation ☐

[1 mark]

2 Which of the following is **not** a religious group which works towards peacemaking?
Put a tick (✓) in the correct box.

- A   Muslim Peace Fellowship ☐
- B   Tearfund® ☐
- C   Campaign for Nuclear Disarmament ☐
- D   Pax Christi ☐

[1 mark]

3 Give two examples of how religious people might support victims of war without visiting the war zone themselves.

1) ....

....

2) ....

....

[2 marks]

4 'Religious people should focus on their own relationship with God before resolving conflicts between others.'

SPaG MARKS

Evaluate this statement. Your answer should include the following:
- religious arguments that support the statement
- religious arguments that disagree with the statement
- a conclusion.

You can also include non-religious points of view in your answer.

Write your answer on a separate sheet of paper.

[12 marks]

Score: ☐ / 16

Theme D — Religion, Peace and Conflict

Theme E — Religion, Crime and Punishment

Law, Crime and Forgiveness

1   Which of the following is often considered a reason for crime in society?
Put a tick (✓) in the correct box.

    A   Wealth   ☐

    B   Compassion   ☐

    C   Poverty   ☐

    D   Justice   ☐

[1 mark]

2   Which of the following means breaking one of God's laws?
Put a tick (✓) in the correct box.

    A   Crime   ☐

    B   Sin   ☐

    C   Judgement   ☐

    D   Restitution   ☐

[1 mark]

3   Give two examples of serious crimes.

1) ....

....

2) ....

....

[2 marks]

4   Explain two contrasting beliefs in British society today about forgiveness.
You must refer to the main religious tradition in the UK and at least one other religious viewpoint.

....

....

....

....

....

[4 marks]

5 Which of the following refers to a person's aim or purpose when they act?
Put a tick (✓) in the correct box.

    A   Sanctity of life ☐

    B   Duty ☐

    C   Chaos ☐

    D   Intention ☐

[1 mark]

6 Explain two religious beliefs about obeying the law.
Your answer should refer to specific religious teachings or sacred texts.

....

....

....

....

....

....

....

[5 marks]

7 'Responsibility for breaking the law lies entirely with the person who commits the crime.'

(SPaG MARKS)

Evaluate this statement. Your answer should include the following:
- religious arguments that support the statement
- religious arguments that disagree with the statement
- a conclusion.

You can also include non-religious points of view in your answer.

Write your answer on a separate sheet of paper.

[12 marks]

Exam Tip

If a 4 mark question on one of the themes refers to 'British society', you need to write about Christianity in your answer (that's the main religious tradition in the UK). You should also mention at least one other religious viewpoint too. Make sure you give contrasting views, if that's what the question wants.

Score ☐ / 26

Theme E — Religion, Crime and Punishment

Punishment and the Death Penalty

1 Which term refers to the principle of creating the best balance of good and bad results? Put a tick (✓) in the correct box.

- A   Sanctity   ☐
- B   Utility   ☐
- C   Counselling   ☐
- D   Severity   ☐

[1 mark]

2 Which term describes the belief that prisoners have certain entitlements which they can never lose, no matter what they have done? Put a tick (✓) in the correct box.

- A   Human Rights   ☐
- B   Corporal Punishment   ☐
- C   Espionage   ☐
- D   Agape   ☐

[1 mark]

3 Give two reasons that religious believers might give to justify punishing criminals.

1) ....

....

2) ....

....

[2 marks]

4 Explain two similar religious beliefs in British society today about the use of the death penalty. You must refer to the main religious tradition in the UK and at least one other religious viewpoint.

....

....

....

....

....

[4 marks]

Theme E — Religion, Crime and Punishment

48

5 Which of the following describes someone who helps a prisoner at the end of their sentence adjust to life outside prison? Put a tick (✓) in the correct box.

    A   Offender   ☐

    B   Judge   ☐

    C   Prophet   ☐

    D   Mentor   ☐

[1 mark]

6 Explain two religious beliefs about corporal punishment.
Your answer should refer to specific religious teachings or sacred texts.

....

....

....

....

....

....

....

[5 marks]

7 'Prison should not be a positive experience.'

(SPaG MARKS)

Evaluate this statement. Your answer should include the following:
- religious arguments that support the statement
- religious arguments that disagree with the statement
- a conclusion.

You can also include non-religious points of view in your answer.

Write your answer on a separate sheet of paper.

[12 marks]

Exam Tip

The exam will only be made up of 1, 2, 4, 5 and 12 mark questions. The more marks that a question is worth, the more you should write and the more time you should spend on it. Try practising answering 1 and 2 mark questions as quickly as possible so that you have lots of time left for the pesky 12 mark-ers.

Score ☐ / 26

Theme E — Religion, Crime and Punishment

Theme F — Religion, Human Rights and Social Justice

Attitudes to Equality

1 Which of the following is the belief that one gender is inferior to another? Put a tick (✓) in the correct box.

- A Sexism ☐
- B Racism ☐
- C Homophobia ☐
- D Maternity ☐

[1 mark]

2 Which act from 2010 makes it illegal to discriminate against people based on certain protected characteristics? Put a tick (✓) in the correct box.

- A The Inequality Act ☐
- B The Freedom of Speech Act ☐
- C The Equality Act ☐
- D The Disability Act ☐

[1 mark]

3 Name two of the 'protected characteristics' that it is illegal to discriminate against in the UK.

1) ....

....

2) ....

....

[2 marks]

4 Explain two similar religious beliefs about gender equality within religion. You must refer to the views of at least one religious group.

....

....

....

....

....

[4 marks]

5 Which of the following terms describes when someone who belongs to a group that's often discriminated against is given an advantage?
Put a tick (✓) in the correct box.

- A Racism ☐
- B Prejudice ☐
- C Negative discrimination ☐
- D Positive discrimination ☐

[1 mark]

6 Explain two religious beliefs about racism.
Your answer should refer to specific religious teachings or sacred texts.

....
....
....
....
....
....

[5 marks]

7 'Religion should lead the way on equality.'   (SPaG MARKS)

Evaluate this statement. Your answer should include the following:
- religious arguments that support the statement
- religious arguments that disagree with the statement
- a conclusion.

You can also include non-religious points of view in your answer.

Write your answer on a separate sheet of paper.

[12 marks]

Exam Tip

You need to be really careful with 4 mark questions. For questions on the Themes, they'll sometimes ask about contrasting views and sometimes ask about similar views. Make sure you answer the question properly — you'll miss out on marks if you write about contrasting views for a 'similar' question, and vice versa.

Score ☐ / 26

Theme F — Religion, Human Rights and Social Justice

Human Rights and Freedom of Belief

1 Which of the following organisations published the Universal Declaration of Human Rights in 1948? Put a tick (✓) in the correct box.

    A   Oxfam ☐

    B   The United Nations ☐

    C   The Roman Catholic Church ☐

    D   Global Freedom Network ☐

[1 mark]

2 Which of the following can describe changing from one faith to another? Put a tick (✓) in the correct box.

    A   Confession ☐

    B   Transformation ☐

    C   Conversion ☐

    D   Agnosticism ☐

[1 mark]

3 Give two religious beliefs about human rights.

1) ....

....

2) ....

....

[2 marks]

4 'Everyone should be free to make their own choices about the religious beliefs they hold.'

Evaluate this statement. Your answer should include the following:
- religious arguments that support the statement
- religious arguments that disagree with the statement
- a conclusion.

You can also include non-religious points of view in your answer.

Write your answer on a separate sheet of paper.

[12 marks]

Score: ☐ / 16

Theme F — Religion, Human Rights and Social Justice

Social Justice, Wealth and Poverty

1 Which of the following is a key idea behind social justice?
Put a tick (✓) in the correct box.

- **A** People can follow any faith. ☐
- **B** People should have the right to a fair trial. ☐
- **C** Criminals should do community service. ☐
- **D** Everyone should be treated fairly. ☐

[1 mark]

2 Which of the following is **not** an organisation that focuses on poverty in developing countries?
Put a tick (✓) in the correct box.

- **A** Amnesty International ☐
- **B** The Fairtrade Foundation ☐
- **C** Tearfund® ☐
- **D** Muslim Aid ☐

[1 mark]

3 Give two causes of poverty that religious believers might try to combat.

1) ....

....

2) ....

....

[2 marks]

4 Give two similar religious beliefs about people-trafficking.
You must refer to the views of at least one religious group.

....

....

....

....

....

[4 marks]

Theme F — Religion, Human Rights and Social Justice

5 Which phrase describes the amount workers should be paid to give them an acceptable standard of living? Put a tick (✓) in the correct box.

- **A** Universal credit ☐
- **B** National living wage ☐
- **C** Salary ☐
- **D** National minimum wage ☐

[1 mark]

6 Explain two religious beliefs about giving money to the poor.
Your answer should refer to specific religious teachings or sacred texts.

....
....
....
....
....
....
....

[5 marks]

7 'Money is not evil in itself.'

(SPaG MARKS)

Evaluate this statement. Your answer should include the following:
- religious arguments that support the statement
- religious arguments that disagree with the statement
- a conclusion.

You can also include non-religious points of view in your answer.

Write your answer on a separate sheet of paper.

[12 marks]

Exam Tip

When you're asked to give or explain two religious beliefs, they don't have to be from the same religion. For 2 mark questions, you can give general views that many different religious believers might share, but for 4 and 5 mark questions, you need to give some more detail to explain who holds those beliefs and why.

Score ☐ / 26

Theme F — Religion, Human Rights and Social Justice

The Start of Jesus's Ministry

1 Which of the following is the name of the man who baptised Jesus?
Put a tick (✓) in the correct box.

- A John ☐
- B Mark ☐
- C Isaiah ☐
- D Joel ☐

[1 mark]

2 Which of the following is how God showed his love for Jesus while he was being tempted in the desert? Put a tick (✓) in the correct box.

- A He spoke to Jesus from the sky ☐
- B He sent Jesus food ☐
- C He sent angels to look after him ☐
- D He forgave Jesus for sinning ☐

[1 mark]

3 Give two reasons why it is important to Christians that Mark calls Jesus 'the Messiah'.

1) ....

....

2) ....

....

[2 marks]

4 'The story of Jesus's baptism is the most important story in Mark's Gospel.'

(SPaG MARKS)

Evaluate this statement. Your answer should include the following:
- references to Mark's Gospel
- arguments that support the statement
- arguments that disagree with the statement
- a conclusion.

Write your answer on a separate sheet of paper.

[12 marks]

Score: ☐ / 16

Jesus's Miracles

1 Which of the following is the person Jairus asked Jesus to heal?
Put a tick (✓) in the correct box.

- A His daughter ☐
- B His son ☐
- C His mother ☐
- D His wife ☐

[1 mark]

2 Explain two contrasting views about the truth of the miracle stories in Mark's Gospel.

....
....
....
....
....

[4 marks]

3 Explain two ways in which the story of Jesus healing the paralysed man is important to Christians today. Your answer should refer to Mark's Gospel.

....
....
....
....
....
....

[5 marks]

Score: ☐
10

Theme G — St Mark's Gospel: the Life of Jesus

The Later Ministry of Jesus

1 Which of the following was **not** one of the replies given by the disciples when Jesus asked them who people said he was? Put a tick (✓) in the correct box.

- A Moses ☐
- B John the Baptist ☐
- C One of the prophets ☐
- D Elijah ☐

[1 mark]

2 Which of the following is the way Jesus entered Jerusalem? Put a tick (✓) in the correct box.

- A On a horse ☐
- B Carrying his cross ☐
- C Walking ☐
- D On a donkey ☐

[1 mark]

3 Give two things that Jesus predicted about his own future in Mark's Gospel.

1) ....

....

2) ....

....

[2 marks]

4 Explain two contrasting views about Jesus's entrance into Jerusalem.

....

....

....

....

....

....

[4 marks]

Theme G — St Mark's Gospel: the Life of Jesus

5 Give two events that happened at the transfiguration.

1) ....

....

2) ....

....

[2 marks]

6 Explain two reasons why the story of James and John's request is important to Christians. Your answer should refer to Mark's Gospel.

....

....

....

....

....

....

....

[5 marks]

7 'Jesus did not see himself as the Messiah, which is why he tried to stop people from giving him that title.'

(SPaG MARKS)

Evaluate this statement. Your answer should include the following:
- references to Mark's Gospel
- arguments that support the statement
- arguments that disagree with the statement
- a conclusion.

Write your answer on a separate sheet of paper.

[12 marks]

Exam Tip

In 5 mark questions, you will be asked to give two points, and you can pick up two marks for each point if you explain it well enough. The fifth mark you can pick up is for referring to St Mark's Gospel — this means giving a direct quotation, or mentioning a specific story or event that's relevant to the point you're making.

Score

27

Theme G — St Mark's Gospel: the Life of Jesus

The Final Days in Jerusalem

1 Which of the following is the reason Pilate offered to release Jesus?
Put a tick (✓) in the correct box.

    A   The chief priests asked him to ☐

    B   It was Passover ☐

    C   He was afraid of the crowd ☐

    D   Barabbas was too dangerous ☐

[1 mark]

2 Which of the following is **not** one of the women who discovered Jesus's empty tomb?
Put a tick (✓) in the correct box.

    A   Salome ☐

    B   Mary Magdalene ☐

    C   Bethany ☐

    D   Mary, mother of James ☐

[1 mark]

3 Give two things that happened at the Last Supper.

1) ....

....

2) ....

....

[2 marks]

4 Explain two contrasting Christian views about the significance of Jesus's crucifixion.

....

....

....

....

....

....

[4 marks]

Theme G — St Mark's Gospel: the Life of Jesus

5 Which of the following happened just after Jesus died on the cross?
Put a tick (✓) in the correct box.

    A   Jesus rose from the dead   ☐

    B   The temple curtain ripped   ☐

    C   A Roman soldier mocked Jesus   ☐

    D   Mary Magdalene began to weep   ☐

[1 mark]

6 Explain two reasons why the events in the Garden of Gethsemane are important for Christians. Your answer should refer to Mark's Gospel.

....

....

....

....

....

....

....

[5 marks]

7 'Jesus voluntarily sacrificed himself for the sake of mankind.'

(SPaG MARKS)

Evaluate this statement. Your answer should include the following:
- references to Mark's Gospel
- arguments that support the statement
- arguments that disagree with the statement
- a conclusion.

Write your answer on a separate sheet of paper.

[12 marks]

Exam Tip

A lot happened in the last few days of Jesus's life. Make sure you revise what happened during these important days, and when each event happened. It might help to make a timeline of events leading up to his death and resurrection. You can revise by covering up your timeline and trying to recall each event in order.

Score ☐ / 26

Theme G — St Mark's Gospel: the Life of Jesus

The Kingdom of God

1 Which of the following is **not** a reason why many people think Mark's Gospel is an accurate source? Put a tick (✓) in the correct box.

    A   It contains similar information to the other gospels. ☐

    B   It was probably written within 50 years of Jesus's death. ☐

    C   It was written by an anonymous author. ☐

    D   Historians at the time mentioned events from Mark's Gospel. ☐

[1 mark]

2 Which of the following asked Jesus about the most important commandment? Put a tick (✓) in the correct box.

    A   A young child ☐

    B   One of the disciples ☐

    C   A Roman soldier ☐

    D   A teacher of the law ☐

[1 mark]

3 Give two things Christians can learn about the kingdom of God from the parable of the mustard seed.

1) ....

....

2) ....

....

[2 marks]

4 Explain two contrasting views seen in St Marks's Gospel about the status of children.

....

....

....

....

....

[4 marks]

5 Give two things that happen to the seeds in the parable of the sower.

1) ....

....

2) ....

....

[2 marks]

6 Explain two reasons why the story of the rich man is important to modern-day Christians. Your answer should refer to Mark's Gospel.

....

....

....

....

....

....

....

[5 marks]

7 'The kingdom of God means a physical place on earth.'

SPaG MARKS

Evaluate this statement. Your answer should include the following:
- references to Mark's Gospel
- arguments that support the statement
- arguments that disagree with the statement
- a conclusion.

Write your answer on a separate sheet of paper.

[12 marks]

Exam Tip

The kingdom of God is a really important part of Jesus's teaching and he speaks about it many times in Mark's Gospel, explaining what the kingdom of God is like using parables. Make sure you can remember the details he gives, including what he says in reference to the kingdom of God in the different parables.

Score ☐ / 27

Theme H — St Mark's Gospel as a Source of Spiritual Truths

People Disregarded by Society

1 Which of the following is the name of a serious skin disease that Jesus healed in Mark's Gospel? Put a tick (✓) in the correct box.

    A   Possession ☐

    B   Leprosy ☐

    C   Epilepsy ☐

    D   Paralysis ☐

[1 mark]

2 Which of the following did a woman pour over Jesus's head at Bethany? Put a tick (✓) in the correct box.

    A   Perfume ☐

    B   Water ☐

    C   Vinegar ☐

    D   Wine ☐

[1 mark]

3 Give two reasons why sick or disabled people were excluded from first century society.

1) ....

....

2) ....

....

[2 marks]

4 Explain two contrasting views about the story of Jesus driving out a demon from a boy.

....

....

....

....

....

....

[4 marks]

Theme H — St Mark's Gospel as a Source of Spiritual Truths

5 Which of the following did the man with leprosy do after Jesus had healed him?
Put a tick (✓) in the correct box.

    A   He asked Jesus to forgive his sins. ☐

    B   He knelt down in front of Jesus and wept. ☐

    C   He went to tell his family he was cured. ☐

    D   He told everyone what had happened. ☐

[1 mark]

6 Explain two ways in which the story of Jesus healing the Gentile woman's daughter is important to Christians today. Your answer should refer to Mark's Gospel.

....

....

....

....

....

....

[5 marks]

7 'Jesus's treatment of the poor and sick is the most important part of his teaching.'

(SPaG MARKS)

Evaluate this statement. Your answer should include the following:
- references to Mark's Gospel
- arguments that support the statement
- arguments that disagree with the statement
- a conclusion.

Write your answer on a separate sheet of paper.

[12 marks]

Exam Tip

Multiple choice questions are a great way of picking up marks, and they'll give you confidence at the beginning of each section of the exam paper. Just make sure you read all the options really carefully before you choose your answer — you don't want to lose marks by trying to race through the questions too quickly.

Score ☐ / 26

Theme H — St Mark's Gospel as a Source of Spiritual Truths

Faith and Discipleship

1 Which of the following is the reason Jesus healed the woman with a haemorrhage?
Put a tick (✓) in the correct box.

- A   She had faith ☐
- B   He pitied her ☐
- C   She begged him to ☐
- D   The crowd asked him to ☐

[1 mark]

2 Which of the following is **not** something Jesus's disciples did when he sent them out to other places? Put a tick (✓) in the correct box.

- A   Preach the Gospel ☐
- B   Drive out demons ☐
- C   Heal the sick ☐
- D   Walk on water ☐

[1 mark]

3 Give the names of two of Jesus's disciples who were originally fishermen.

1) ....

2) ....

[2 marks]

4 Explain two contrasting beliefs about Peter's denial of Jesus.

....

....

....

....

....

[4 marks]

Theme H — St Mark's Gospel as a Source of Spiritual Truths

5 Which of the following is a meaning of the word 'disciple'?
Put a tick (✓) in the correct box.

    A   Pupil   ☐

    B   Teacher   ☐

    C   Someone who follows rules   ☐

    D   Friend   ☐

[1 mark]

6 Explain two ways in which the idea of discipleship found in Mark's Gospel is important to Christians today. Your answer should refer to Mark's Gospel.

....

....

....

....

....

....

....

[5 marks]

7 'People who live a good life will go to heaven, even if they are not Christian.'

(SPaG MARKS)

Evaluate this statement. Your answer should include the following:
- references to Mark's Gospel
- arguments that support the statement
- arguments that disagree with the statement
- a conclusion.

Write your answer on a separate sheet of paper.

[12 marks]

Exam Tip

Always read 12 mark questions carefully — they'll tell you what to include in your answer. If it tells you to reference Mark's Gospel, then you need to in order to get top marks. Don't lose out on marks by not reading the question carefully enough. Remember you'll get marks for spelling, punctuation and grammar too.

Score ☐ / 26

Theme H — St Mark's Gospel as a Source of Spiritual Truths

2 Mark Questions

In this section, you get to be the examiner. You'll look at some students' answers to exam questions and decide what marks they should get. It'll help you understand what the examiners are looking for — which will improve the quality of your answers. Here's how it works:

1. Read each question and the information about how to mark it.
2. You don't have to answer the questions. Instead, there are some sample student answers for each question — it's your job to mark them.
3. For each answer, use the marking guidance to decide how many marks it's worth.

Marking Guidance for 2 Mark Questions

1) 2 mark questions test basic knowledge of beliefs and practices. Two correct points are needed to get full marks.

2) The answers don't need a detailed explanation — a short sentence or phrase, or sometimes just a word, is enough to get the mark for each point.

3) Marking answers to these questions is pretty simple — just give 1 mark for each correct point. Remember, only 2 marks are available in total — so only two correct points can count.

Sample 2 Mark Question

Have a read of this question, then read the list of possible answers given below it.
Once you've done that, you'll be ready to mark the sample answers on the next page.

Give two of the Ten Obligatory Acts in Shi'a Islam.

This question is on Islam.

1) ....

....

2) ....

....

[2 marks]

Here is a list of facts a correct answer could include:

- Prayer (salah)
- Charitable giving (zakah)
- The obligation to fast during Ramadan (sawm)
- Pilgrimage to Makkah (hajj)
- Paying an annual tax of 20% to charity in addition to zakah (khums)
- Striving to live a good life and defend Islam (jihad)
- To encourage good deeds (amr-bil-maroof)
- To avoid bad deeds (nahi anil munkar)
- To love those who follow Allah (tawalla)
- To not associate with enemies of Allah (tabarra)

When answers include specialist terms, it's okay to answer in either the original language (Arabic) or English.

Answer 1

1) Salah

2) Every Muslim should take a pilgrimage to Makkah every year (if they can afford it and are healthy enough).

This answer gets **1** mark(s) out of 2 because point 1) is correct, but point 2) is wrong — Muslims are only encouraged to take the pilgrimage at least once in their lifetime.

You can write notes around the answers, e.g. ticking and crossing the different facts.

Make sure you give reasons for your marking.

Answer 2

1) Shi'a Muslims are obligated to fast during Ramadan. This is known as sawm.

2) They are encouraged to give charitably to wherever they choose. They also pay an annual tax of 20% of profits to charity.

This answer gets ☐ mark(s) out of 2 because ....

Answer 3

1) They say grace before eating a meal.

2) Shi'a Muslims are obligated to encourage good deeds.

This answer gets ☐ mark(s) out of 2 because ....

Marking Guidance and Practice

4 Mark Questions

Marking Guidance for 4 Mark Questions

1) 4 mark questions require <u>two detailed points</u> for full marks. In the 'Beliefs' part of Paper 1, they ask about two ways in which a particular belief <u>influences</u> people. In the 'Practices' part of Paper 1, and in Paper 2, they ask about two <u>similar</u> or <u>contrasting</u> beliefs, practices or viewpoints.

2) 4 mark questions always start with 'Explain two...'. It's not enough to write down two basic ideas — each point should contain a <u>well-developed explanation</u>. This might be extra details about the belief or practice, or reasons why a particular belief is held.

3) Use these guidelines when marking answers to 4 mark questions:

- Marks can be awarded for up to two correct points.
- For each correct point, award 2 marks if they've given a detailed explanation. Award 1 mark if they've only given a simple explanation.
- Make sure the answer actually answers the question. If the question asks how a belief influences people, the answer must discuss influences, not just the belief itself. If the question asks for similar points, the second point can only receive marks if it's similar to the first one. For a contrasting question, the second point must contain a contrasting idea to the first.
- Some 4 mark questions specify that the views of the main religious tradition in the UK (Christianity) must be discussed. For these questions, a maximum of 2 marks can be awarded if no Christian viewpoints have been given.

Sample 4 Mark Question

> Explain two contrasting beliefs about animal experimentation. You must refer to the views of at least one religious group.
>
> *This question is on Theme B.*
>
> *[4 marks]*

Here's a summary of some ideas that could be included in a correct answer. They'd need explaining in more detail in the actual answer:

Christianity

- Some Christians believe humans have dominion over animals, so they can use them for their own benefit.
- The Roman Catholic Church says animal testing should be allowed, but only where it's needed to help protect human life, e.g. for testing medicine.
- Quakers think it is always wrong to cause suffering to animals.

Islam

- Many Muslims are against testing cosmetics on animals, because they believe the role of khalifah means they should care for animals.
- Many believe experimentation should be allowed for medical research, if there's no alternative.

Marking Guidance and Practice

Answer 1

Muslims will generally allow animal testing if it is done to produce genuine medical advances for humans and if there is no alternative. They do however believe that the animals involved in the testing should always be treated humanely, and no unnecessary pain should be inflicted on them.

By contrast, some Christians believe it is always wrong to experiment on animals, even if it is for the benefit of medical advances. For example, many Quakers believe that any ill-treatment of animals is wrong, no matter what. They believe the principle of stewardship means that all animals should be cared for and looked after as God's creations.

This answer gets [ ] mark(s) out of 4 because ....

....

....

....

Answer 2

Some Christians agree with animal experimentation in some circumstances. They believe in dominion, which means that humans can do what they want with animals. This would include experimenting on animals to make scientific advances, for example.

Muslims believe that when animals are killed for food, they should be killed humanely. Only then would the meat be considered halal.

This answer gets [ ] mark(s) out of 4 because ....

....

....

....

Marking Guidance and Practice

5 Mark Questions

Marking Guidance for 5 Mark Questions

1) 5 mark questions are similar to 4 mark questions — they always start with 'Explain two...', and a good answer must include <u>two well-explained points</u>.

2) 5 mark questions are quite straightforward — they just ask about two <u>beliefs</u> (there's <u>no requirement</u> for the points to be either similar or contrasting).

3) The important thing to remember is that to get full marks, an answer to a 5 mark question must include a reference to a <u>specific religious teaching</u> or <u>sacred text</u>.

4) This can be a direct quote, or the teaching can be paraphrased.

5) The answer must say where the teaching <u>comes from</u>, e.g. the Bible, Qur'an, etc.

6) Use these <u>guidelines</u> when marking answers to 5 mark questions:

> - Marks can be awarded for up to two correct points.
> - For each correct point, award 2 marks if they've given a detailed explanation. Award 1 mark if they've only given a simple explanation.
> - Award 1 additional mark if the answer contains a suitable and correct reference to a sacred text or specific religious teaching.

Sample 5 Mark Question

> Explain two religious beliefs about the importance of peace.
> Your answer should refer to specific religious teachings or sacred texts.
>
> *This question is on Theme D.*
>
> [5 marks]

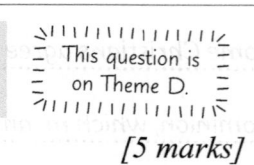

A summary of some ideas that could be included in a correct answer is given below. The answer itself would require more detailed explanation, plus a reference to a teaching or sacred text for full marks.

Christianity
- Jesus described those that make peace as "blessed" in the Sermon on the Mount.
- Jesus is sometimes described as the "Prince of Peace".
- Jesus said to turn the other cheek if violence is used against you.

Islam
- The Qur'an says good Muslims respond peacefully to provocation and do not retaliate with violence.
- Islam teaches that war is sometimes necessary, but Muslims should work to achieve peace wherever possible.

Marking Guidance and Practice

Answer 1

> Peace is very important for Christians as they believe that God prefers people to be peaceful instead of violent. Jesus said "Love your enemies".
>
> Peace is also very important for Muslims and this is shown when they pray or help people from other religions in the community.

This answer gets ☐ mark(s) out of 5 because ....

....

....

....

....

Answer 2

> Muslims believe it is very important to live peacefully and to promote peace in the world. While Islam teaches that violence is sometimes justified, it's more important to promote peace and non-violence, even in the face of violence and aggression. The Qur'an says, "The true servants of the Most Compassionate are those who walk on the earth humbly, and when the foolish address them improperly, they only respond with peace".
>
> Peace is also a very important idea in Christianity. Jesus taught that peace is the ultimate goal, and Christians believe that God wanted him to create peace on Earth. Christians would therefore want to follow Jesus's example, and would see it as important to seek peace and avoid conflict.

This answer gets ☐ mark(s) out of 5 because ....

....

....

....

....

Marking Guidance and Practice

12 Mark Questions

Marking Guidance for 12 Mark Questions

1) A good answer to a 12 mark question is an <u>extended</u> piece of writing, explaining a number of points that both <u>support</u> and <u>argue against</u> the statement given in the question. It should also have a carefully considered <u>conclusion</u>.

2) The mark scheme for 12 mark questions is broken down into <u>different levels</u>, as shown below. When marking, you should decide which level <u>best describes</u> the answer, and then decide whether the answer <u>deserves</u> a lower or higher mark within the given range, based on the <u>quality</u> of the <u>explanations</u> and <u>reasoning</u>.

- Level 0: There is no relevant information. *[0 marks]*
- Level 1: The answer contains one point of view, with one or more reasons given to support it. *[1-3 marks]*
- Level 2: A careful consideration of one point of view is given. The response should be logical and well-reasoned, demonstrating knowledge and understanding of evidence for that point of view.
  OR
  The answer contains more than one point of view.
  One or more reasons are given in support of each.
  [4-6 marks]
- Level 3: A careful consideration of more than one point of view is given. The response should be logical and well-reasoned, demonstrating knowledge and understanding of evidence for each point of view. There must be a clear reference to one or more religions. *[7-9 marks]*
- Level 4: A well-argued answer, with careful consideration of more than one point of view and a conclusion. The response should be logical and well-reasoned, demonstrating knowledge and understanding of evidence for each point of view. There must be clear references to one or more religions. *[10-12 marks]*

Sample 12 Mark Question

'Jesus's death had to happen in order to save humanity.'

Evaluate this statement. Your answer should include the following:
- examples from Christian teachings
- arguments that support the statement
- arguments that disagree with the statement
- a conclusion.

This question is on Christianity.

[12 marks]

Marking Guidance and Practice

A summary of some ideas that could be included in a correct answer is given below. The answer itself would require more detailed explanation, a careful consideration of different sides of the argument, and a conclusion.

Arguments that support the statement:

- All humans sin — everyone is born with 'original sin'.
- Since God is just, sin must be punished. To save humankind from this punishment, God allowed his Son to die on the cross, to pay for the sins of humanity.
- Jesus's death reconciled humanity with God — known as the atonement.

Arguments that disagree with the statement:

- God is loving and all-powerful. He would not require Jesus's death in order to forgive people's sins.
- Jesus's ministry taught humanity how it could be free from sin. This alone can save humankind.
- Jesus's death happened for different reasons. It showed God's love for humans, as Jesus was willing to suffer like they do. Jesus's resurrection showed God's power over death.

Answer 1

Some Christians would agree that Jesus did have to die to save humanity. This is because in the Bible it says that God sent Jesus to Earth to save human beings from sin.

Sometimes Jesus is called the 'lamb of God' because lambs were sacrificed and Jesus was a sacrifice for humans. If Jesus didn't die to save humanity, then why did he die? It would not make sense.

Other Christians would disagree and say that Jesus didn't have to die to save humanity. Christians believe that God is omnipotent, which means that he can do anything and there are no limits on his power. This is shown in Genesis when he says "Let there be light" and creates all light. If God wanted to save humanity then he could just do it.

This answer gets [ ] mark(s) out of 12 because...

Marking Guidance and Practice

Answer 2

Some Christians would agree with this view as they would argue that Jesus's crucifixion and death were necessary to atone for the sins of humanity. This is because Christianity teaches that humanity is in need of being saved. The book of Genesis says that sin entered the world when Adam and Eve misused free will and this resulted in the Fall. St Augustine called this original sin. As a result of original sin and the continuing misuse of free will, humanity is justifiably separated from God as punishment. However, Christians also believe that God is both loving and just, and so ensured that there was a way for humanity to be reconciled with Him. This is through the sacrifice and death of his son, Jesus. Christians believe that when Jesus died he paid the debt of human sin, allowing for those with faith to be saved and redeemed: "For God so loved the world that he gave his one and only Son, that whoever believes in him shall not perish but have eternal life" (John 3). Without Jesus's death, the debt of sin could not be paid and humanity could not be saved.

Other Christians would disagree with this statement. They might argue that, as an omnipotent being, God would be able to save humanity through some other way, without Jesus dying. However, God chose to save humanity this way in order to show his love for humanity. By existing as the incarnation, God experienced suffering and death in the same way as people do. In the same way, through Jesus's death and resurrection afterwards, God was showing how, ultimately, life will win over death. God didn't have to do this, but he chose to.

In conclusion, both arguments are strong but the first view seems more persuasive. If God is just, as well as loving and powerful, it seems that a sin needs to be paid for. If sinning against God is infinitely bad, then it makes sense that only an infinitely precious sacrifice could balance that debt. So, it does seem likely that Jesus's death had to happen to save humanity.

This answer gets [ ] mark(s) out of 12 because ....

Marking Guidance and Practice

Answers

Mark Schemes

The answers provided here are just examples of points you could make. Other answers are acceptable, as long as they are relevant and correct.

Use this mark scheme for all 4 mark questions:
- *Marks can be awarded for up to two correct points.*
- *For each correct point, award 2 marks for a detailed explanation, or 1 mark for a simple explanation.*
- *If the question asks how a belief influences people, the answer must discuss influences, not just the belief itself. If the question asks for similar points, the second point can only receive marks if it's similar to the first one. For a contrasting question, the second point must contain a contrasting idea to the first.*
- *If the question specifies that the views of the main religious tradition in the UK (Christianity) must be discussed, a maximum of 2 marks can be awarded if no Christian viewpoints have been given.*

Use this mark scheme for all 5 mark questions:
- *Marks can be awarded for up to two correct points.*
- *For each correct point, award 2 marks for a detailed explanation, or 1 mark for a simple explanation.*
- *Award 1 additional mark if the answer contains a suitable and correct reference to a sacred text or specific religious teaching.*

12 mark questions are level marked — read the level descriptions below, and work out which level best suits the answer. Then decide whether the answer deserves a lower or higher mark within the range, depending on the quality of the answer.

Use this mark scheme for all 12 mark questions:

Level 0: There is no relevant information. *[0 marks]*

Level 1: The answer contains one point of view, with one or more reasons given to support it. *[1-3 marks]*

Level 2: A careful consideration of one point of view is given. The response should be logical and well-reasoned, demonstrating knowledge and understanding of evidence for that point of view. *[4-6 marks]*
OR The answer contains more than one point of view. One or more reasons are given in support of each. *[4-6 marks]*

Level 3: A careful consideration of more than one point of view is given. The response should be logical and well-reasoned, demonstrating knowledge and understanding of evidence for each point of view. There must be a clear reference to one or more religions. *[7-9 marks]*

Level 4: A well-argued answer, with careful consideration of more than one point of view and a conclusion. The response should be logical and well-reasoned, demonstrating knowledge and understanding of evidence for each point of view. There must be clear references to one or more religions. *[10-12 marks]*

Some 12 mark questions have 3 extra marks available for spelling punctuation and grammar. This is highlighted on the relevant questions — use this mark scheme to award marks for spelling, punctuation and grammar:

[3 marks] for accurate spelling, punctuation and grammar throughout, including correct spelling and use of a wide range of specialist terms.

[2 marks] for generally accurate spelling, punctuation and grammar. A good range of specialist terms are used correctly.

[1 mark] for reasonably accurate spelling, punctuation and grammar. Limited range of specialist terms used.

[0 marks] for no response, an answer that is not relevant to the question, or one in which the spelling, punctuation and grammar are so poor that the meaning is unclear.

Beliefs, Teachings and Practices — Christianity and Catholic Christianity

Page 3 — The Nature of God

1. The Father is the most important person of the Trinity *[1 mark]*.

2. Immanent *[1 mark]*

3. - (Roman) Catholicism
   - Protestantism (or any Protestant denominations, e.g. Anglicanism, Methodism, Baptists, Evangelicalism, Presbyterianism)
   - Orthodox/Eastern Orthodox
   [2 marks available, 1 mark for each correct point]

4. Arguments that support the statement:
   - Believing in the Trinity means believing that Jesus is divine. This belief is necessary to understand how the story of Jesus's death and resurrection, as told in the Gospels, leads to the salvation of Christians. So without an understanding of the Trinity, Christian belief is impossible.
   - A belief in the Trinity is the only way that Christians can make sense of what God is like in the Bible, the main text of the religion. The Father is the God of the Old Testament who created the universe and spoke to Adam, Abraham and Moses. The Son is Jesus who lived as a human being on earth. The Holy Spirit is the unseen presence of God that guides people.
   - The idea of the Trinity was a major issue at the Councils of Nicaea and Constantinople, and a description of it makes up the Nicene Creed. This shows how important the belief is to Christians.

   Arguments against the statement:
   - Some Christians, like Christadelphians and Jehovah's Witnesses, do not believe in the Trinity. However, they still consider themselves Christians, which shows that this belief is not the most important for all Christians.
   - Belief in the salvation of mankind through Jesus's death on the cross is more important than a belief in the Trinity. Without it, the religion would not exist. It is possible to believe that Jesus was the Son of God without believing in the Trinity.
   - There is no direct reference to the Trinity in the Bible, although the Father, the Son and the Holy Spirit are all referred to. This suggests that the Trinity is not the most important belief for Christians, because there are other teachings which appear repeatedly in the Bible like Jesus's teachings on the kingdom of God or the importance of loving others.
   [12 marks available — see p.75 for mark scheme]

Page 4 — Creation

1. Land animals were created on the same day as people *[1 mark]*.

2. - God created humans "in his own image" (Genesis 1:27 NIV). This means that humans are special when compared to the rest of creation, so they should all be treated with respect.
   - Since humans are created in God's image, they should try to be more like God — they should be benevolent and just.
   - God created Adam and Eve individually — he made Adam from dust and Eve from Adam's rib. Christians believe that this shows God's special love for human beings, and the personal relationship they can have with him.
   [4 marks available — see p.75 for mark scheme]

3. - The creation story describes how God "created the heavens and the earth" (Genesis 1:1 NIV) in only six days. This demonstrates to Christians that God is omnipotent — all powerful.
   - In order to create the universe, Christians argue that God must have existed before it. This shows that he is eternal, as he existed before time began.
   - God created the universe, and he "saw that it was good" (Genesis 1:25 NIV). He then created human beings to "rule over" his creation (Genesis 1:26 NIV). To Christians, this shows God's goodness — his benevolence — since he gave humans such an amazing gift.

- The creation story in Genesis says that God created the universe in six days, and then he rested on the seventh. Some Christians interpret this story literally, and so they do not accept the scientific view that the universe has developed over billions of years.
- Some Christians do not think the creation story is literally true — instead they believe that it is symbolic. It helps them to understand what God is like, but they are open to other theories about how the world came to be (like evolution and the Big Bang theory).
[5 marks available — see p.75 for mark scheme]

Page 5 — Evil and Suffering

1. Evil is always more powerful than good *[1 mark]*.
2. Original sin *[1 mark]*
3. - When God created the world, it was purely good.
   - When Adam and Eve disobeyed God, evil came into the world. This is known as 'the Fall'.
   - Adam and Eve were tempted by Satan, who is evil.
   - God created humans with free will, so they can choose whether or not to commit evil.
   [2 marks available, 1 mark for each correct point]
4. Arguments that support the statement:
   - Christians believe that God is omnipotent and benevolent. This means that he has the power to stop natural evil from occurring, and that he should want to do this. The fact that evil still takes place shows that God cannot be both of those things, so the Christian God cannot exist.
   - If suffering exists for a purpose, for example to test people's faith, there are other ways that this could be done without large amounts of terrible suffering.
   - God might not be the cause of moral evil, which comes from humanity's free will, but he should be powerful enough to stop the suffering that comes from it. If he does not, then he cannot be benevolent.
   Arguments against the statement:
   - Humans cannot understand the ways of God. There might be a reason why the Christian God allows evil to take place, but we cannot understand it. Isaiah says, "As the heavens are higher than the earth, so are my ways higher than your ways and my thoughts than your thoughts." (Isaiah 55:9 NIV)
   - Some Christians believe that suffering is a test of faith. James says that Christians should welcome suffering because "the testing of your faith produces perseverance" (James 1:3 NIV). Some Christians believe that people who experience suffering on earth will also be rewarded in heaven if they keep their faith strong.
   - Christians believe that evil entered the world when Adam and Eve used their free will to disobey God in the book of Genesis. By stopping suffering as a result of moral evil, God would be taking away the free will of human beings.
   [12 marks available — see p.75 for mark scheme]

Page 6 — The Afterlife

1. Purgatory *[1 mark]*
2. - Christians believe that after death humans will be judged by God and be sent either to heaven or hell. This means that Christians should try to do good deeds in their lives so they will be sent to heaven.
   - Christians believe that Jesus died on the cross so their sins can be forgiven and they can go to heaven. They therefore pray to Jesus for forgiveness if they have sinned.
   - Christians believe all people will be judged — this encourages some to try to convert non-believers to Christianity, so they have the chance to get to heaven.
   [4 marks available — see p.75 for mark scheme]
3. - If someone believes in Jesus and follows his teachings, their soul will not die but will live forever in heaven: "The one who believes in me will live, even though they die" (John 11:25 NIV).
   - Some Christians believe that heaven is not a real place, but a state of mind. Heaven is closeness to God, whereas hell is separation from him. The Catechism of the Catholic Church (1024) says that "this communion of life and love with the Trinity… is called 'heaven'".

- Christians who get to heaven will live there eternally. John's Gospel says that God sacrificed his son, Jesus, so that "whoever believes in him shall not perish but have eternal life" (John 3:16 NIV).
- Heaven is a desirable place to be — it is paradise. In Luke's Gospel, Jesus tells a criminal he is being crucified beside that "today you will be with me in paradise" (Luke 23:43 NIV).
[5 marks available — see p.75 for mark scheme]

Pages 7-8 — Jesus Christ and Salvation

1. God becoming human *[1 mark]*
2. Grace *[1 mark]*
3. - Jesus rose from the Earth to heaven to be with God.
   - Jesus had finished his mission on Earth, so he could return to heaven.
   - He went to prepare a place for his followers in heaven.
   - It shows how powerful Jesus was — he rose to sit at God's right hand.
   [2 marks available, 1 mark for each correct point]
4. - Christians believe that Jesus was the incarnation of God — God in human form. This leads them to look at Jesus's actions as an example that they should follow in their own lives.
   - The belief that Jesus is the Son of God leads Christians to be thankful to God because they realise how much he must love them to have sent his own son to die for them.
   - If Jesus is the Son of God, this means his words have more authority than those of prophets or other religious leaders. This leads Christians to study them and follow them very closely.
   [4 marks available — see p.75 for mark scheme]
5. - Christians believe redemption is when their sins are forgiven.
   - Christians believe that they can be redeemed because Jesus died on the cross.
   - Jesus's death can redeem all people because he was without sin.
   - In order to be redeemed, Christians must have faith in Jesus.
   [2 marks available, 1 mark for each correct point]
6. - Christianity teaches that after his crucifixion, Jesus rose from the dead: "Why do you look for the living among the dead? He is not here; he has risen!" (Luke 24:5-6 NIV). This shows that Jesus must be the Son of God because he has power over death.
   - The resurrection of Jesus proves that the afterlife exists since he came back from the dead. It gives Christians hope that they will be resurrected after death too. John's Gospel says, "whoever believes in him shall not perish but have eternal life" (John 3:16 NIV).
   - Christians believe that, after death, humans are resurrected and judged. In 2 Corinthians it says that we will be judged "so that each of us may receive what is due to us" for the things we did while alive (2 Corinthians 5:10 NIV).
   - Some Christians believe that our physical bodies will be raised from the dead, but they will be perfected. "The body that is sown is perishable, it is raised imperishable" (1 Corinthians 15:42 NIV). It is these perfect bodies which will live eternally in heaven.
   [5 marks available — see p.75 for mark scheme]
7. Arguments that support the statement:
   - Just before he died, Jesus cried out, asking why God had abandoned him. This shows how much pain and suffering he was going through. This means that he can understand the pain and suffering experienced by humans, which is an important source of comfort for Christians.
   - The idea of original sin — that all humans are born with sin as a result of Adam and Eve's disobedience — means that all humans need God's forgiveness to enter heaven. Jesus's death on the cross allows this forgiveness to take place.
   - Jesus's death on the cross is the most important Christian belief because it shows that God loves mankind so much that he was willing to sacrifice his only son to save us: "For God so loved the world that he gave his one and only Son" (John 3:16 NIV).
   Arguments against the statement:
   - Jesus's resurrection is just as important as his death because it proves that Jesus has power over death — "death no longer has mastery over him" (Romans 6:9 NIV). It gives Christians hope that they will also be resurrected after death and live in heaven with God.

- For their sins to be forgiven, Christians need to have faith that Jesus is the Son of God. This fact is proved by Jesus's resurrection, so it gives Christians the faith they need.
- Jesus's resurrection is proof that Jesus is the Son of God, and therefore Christians should follow his example as described in the Gospels. Jesus told his disciples "I have set you an example that you should do as I have done for you" (John 13:15 NIV). This is more important than his death, which doesn't help Christians decide how to act.
- Jesus's resurrection is more important because without it, Christians' faith in Jesus is pointless as their sins cannot be forgiven. The Bible says, "And if Christ has not been raised, your faith is futile; you are still in your sins" (1 Corinthians 15:17 NIV).
[12 marks available — see p.75 for mark scheme]

Pages 9-10 — Worship and Prayer

1. Supplication *[1 mark]*
2. A baptism *[1 mark]*
3. - Using the rosary helps them to think about events in Jesus's life while praying.
   - They repeat set prayers while holding it. This helps them concentrate.
   - Catholics use the beads to count the number of prayers they have said.
   [2 marks available, 1 mark for each correct point]
4. Viewpoints that see Christians as closer to God in public worship:
   - Some Christians believe that they can become closer to God during public worship because in Matthew's Gospel, Jesus said that he would be present when groups of people worshipped him.
   - Public worship might involve the Eucharist (Holy Communion), which re-enacts Christ's last supper. Many Christians believe eating the bread and drinking the wine brings them close to God.
   Viewpoints that see Christians as closer to God in private worship:
   - Some Christians believe that they can become closer to God during private worship because they can worship in whatever way they think is appropriate at the time.
   - Worshipping privately might allow Christians to worship more often, keeping them closer to God in their daily lives.
   [4 marks available — see p.75 for mark scheme]
5. Pictures of Jesus's suffering *[1 mark]*
6. - The Lord's Prayer was how Jesus taught his disciples to pray in the gospels of Luke and Matthew, saying "This, then, is how you should pray" (Matthew 6:9 NIV), so Christians believe it is important that they also recite it.
   - Christians all over the world and at different points in history have recited the Lord's Prayer, so it makes Christians feel connected to a wider community of worshippers.
   - The Lord's Prayer is accepted by all Christian denominations and is said during church services all over the world. For example, it is in the Church of England's 'Book of Common Prayer'. It helps different denominations remember to focus on what they have in common rather than the disagreements that divide them.
   - The Lord's Prayer includes several different types of prayer. For example, "hallowed be your name" is adoration (Matthew 6:9 NIV) and "Give us today our daily bread" is supplication (Matthew 6:11 NIV). It acts as a reminder of what prayer is for, and how Christians should address God.
   [5 marks available — see p.75 for mark scheme]
7. Arguments that support the statement:
   - Jesus said that instead of praying in full view of everyone else, people should "go into your room, close the door" (Matthew 6:6 NIV) and pray in private. Private prayer is often more informal, as people can have a personal conversation with God. This means that informal prayer is more important to Christians, because it makes it easier to follow Jesus's instructions in Matthew to pray privately.
   - Paul writes, "I want the men everywhere to pray, lifting up holy hands" (1 Timothy 2:8 NIV). This suggests that prayer shouldn't be structured and formal — people should pray whenever they want to.
   - Some Christians argue that informal prayers are more important because they are part of an individual's personal relationship with God. They are a form of private communication which is more natural when it is informal.
   Arguments against the statement:
   - Formal prayer can be more important because it often happens in groups. Jesus said that "where two or three gather in my name, there am I with them" (Matthew 18:20 NIV). When Christians gather for formal church services, Jesus is present.
   - Some formal prayers are performed all around the world, which gives Christians a sense of community. This can offer them comfort when they are suffering.
   - Formal prayers often include all of the different types of prayer — thanksgiving, adoration, confession, supplication and intercession. These different types are important for believers' relationship with God and with other Christians, so it is important to include them regularly. Formal prayer makes sure this happens.
   [12 marks available — see p.75 for mark scheme]

Pages 11-12 — The Sacraments

1. Confirmation *[1 mark]*
2. The Last Supper *[1 mark]*
3. Baptism, the Eucharist (Holy Communion)
   [2 marks available, 1 mark for each correct point]
4. Viewpoints that are in favour of infant baptism:
   - Infant baptism is a good thing because it welcomes the child into the Christian Church.
   - Infant baptism is a good thing because all humans are born with original sin, and baptism cleanses them of it.
   Viewpoints that are in favour of adult baptism:
   - It is better to baptise Christians as adults when they can choose Christianity for themselves.
   - Jesus was baptised as an adult, so Christians should follow his example.
   [4 marks available — see p.75 for mark scheme]
5. Anointing *[1 mark]*
6. - Catholics believe that this sacrament allows the Holy Spirit to strengthen the sick person's faith and help them cope with their current illness (Catechism of the Catholic Church 1532).
   - Catholics believe that anointing the sick links the sick person with Jesus's suffering (Catechism of the Catholic Church 1532). Remembering that Jesus suffered can help sick people endure their own suffering.
   - The Catechism of the Catholic Church (1210) says that all of the seven sacraments are hugely important in a Christian's life — they "give birth and increase, healing and mission to the Christian's life of faith".
   - The Catechism of the Catholic Church (1210) states that "Christ instituted the sacraments of the new law" — Christians perform them in order to follow Jesus's example. Also, when Jesus sent out his disciples they "anointed with oil many people who were ill and healed them" (Mark 6:13 NIV). Catholics follow this example by performing this sacrament.
   [5 marks available — see p.75 for mark scheme]
7. Arguments that support the statement:
   - Some Christians believe that the bread and wine at the Eucharist (Holy Communion) turn into the real body and blood of Christ. The Eucharist is a re-enactment of the suffering and death of Jesus, which then brings the power of Jesus's salvation into their bodies as they consume the bread and wine.
   - The fact that ordinary bread and wine become the body of Jesus is a miracle, which strengthens the faith of those who believe in it. It adds to the proof that Jesus is the Son of God.
   - The Catechism of the Catholic Church (1335) argues that the bread turning into Jesus's body and the wine turning into Jesus's blood echo the miracles of the feeding of the 5000 and Jesus turning water into wine. This links the Eucharist to the events of the Gospel even more strongly, linking the actions of modern Christians with the actions of Jesus during his life.

Arguments against the statement:
- Many Christians believe that the bread and wine do not literally become the body and blood of Jesus, but that the Eucharist is still a very important ceremony because it is a re-enactment of the Last Supper — the final meal Jesus shared with his disciples before his crucifixion.
- According to the Catechism of the Catholic Church (1334), the Eucharist is also important because it links Jesus to events in the Old Testament. The Last Supper took place on Passover, and the bread represents the manna that God gave the Israelites in the desert.
- Some Christians, such as Baptists, believe that the importance of the Eucharist is in Christians coming together as a community to celebrate Jesus's sacrifice. The bread and wine are simply symbols of Jesus's body being broken on the cross, and his blood being spilt as he died.
[12 marks available — see p.75 for mark scheme]

Page 13 — Pilgrimage
1 Jesus and his parents' journey to Jerusalem *[1 mark]*
2 To preach the Gospel *[1 mark]*
3 Lourdes, Walsingham, Lindisfarne, Iona, Taizé, Rome, Jerusalem
   [2 marks available, 1 mark for each correct point]
4 Arguments that support the statement:
   - In recent years, shrines like Lourdes have become very commercialised and busy. Some Christians argue that they will be closer to God if they stay at home and go on an inner journey of faith instead.
   - Some Christians argue that God is omnipresent — in Jeremiah, he asks "Do not I fill heaven and earth?" (Jeremiah 23:24 NIV). This suggests that there is no need to travel to get closer to him.
   - There are no passages in the New Testament which tell Christians to go on pilgrimages, so some Christians argue that they are not important.
   Arguments against the statement:
   - Many Catholics consider pilgrimage to be important because it represents people's journey towards God. In the Catechism of the Catholic Church (2691), it says that pilgrimages "evoke our earthly journey toward heaven".
   - Some Christians go on pilgrimages to escape everyday life and concentrate on their faith in peace. For example, they might go to Taizé or Iona. Modern life can be very fast-paced and hectic, so pilgrimages to calm locations are arguably more important to Christians today.
   - The large number of people visiting shrines like Lourdes proves that pilgrimage remains important to Christians in the modern day. They still travel to distant locations in the hope that they will be healed or their faith will be strengthened.
   [12 marks available — see p.75 for mark scheme]

Page 14 — Christmas and Easter
1 Ash Wednesday *[1 mark]*
2 Viewpoints that support the importance of Christmas:
   - Christmas is a very important festival for Christians because it marks the birth of Jesus, who is the Son of God and who went on to die for the sins of mankind.
   - In Britain, Christmas is widely celebrated even by non-Christians. This makes it an important opportunity for Christians to explain its origins and spread the good news about Jesus to others.
   Viewpoints that see Christmas as less important:
   - Some Christians feel that Christmas is becoming increasingly secular, with traditions like Father Christmas and the giving of expensive gifts taking over from its religious roots.
   - Easter is the celebration of the death and resurrection of Jesus, which brings about the salvation of mankind. This means that Easter is a more important festival than Christmas.
   [4 marks available — see p.75 for mark scheme]
3 - During Lent, the 40 days before Easter, some Christians fast or choose to give something up. They do this to remember the story in the Gospels of Jesus fasting in the desert for 40 days.
   - On Good Friday, the day Jesus was crucified, Christians go to church services to remember his suffering. Sometimes these services last three hours — according to Mark's Gospel, this was the amount of time the sky was dark just before Jesus died: "At noon, darkness came over the whole land until three in the afternoon" (Mark 15:33).
   - Some churches have services at sunrise on Easter Day to represent Mary Magdalene's discovery of Jesus's empty tomb at sunrise as told in the Gospels.
   - In some churches, a Paschal candle is lit on Easter Day. The light of the candle represents the resurrection of Jesus, who said he was "the light of the world" (John 8:12 NIV).
   [5 marks available — see p.75 for mark scheme]

Pages 15-16 — The Work of the Church
1 CAFOD *[1 mark]*
2 It is difficult for the poor to enter the kingdom of God *[1 mark]*.
3 The Salvation Army, Gideons, Hope UK, Tearfund®
   [2 marks available, 1 mark for each correct point]
4 Viewpoints that support the importance of evangelism:
   - Many Christians believe that they have a duty to spread the gospel because Jesus told his disciples to "Go into all the world and preach the gospel to all creation" (Mark 16:15 NIV). For them, helping to save other people is a major part of their religion.
   - Missionaries believe that evangelism is so important that they are willing to move to distant parts of the world to spread the gospel.
   Viewpoints that see evangelism as less important:
   - Some Christians believe that it is more important to have a good personal relationship with God than to spend time spreading the word about him to others.
   - Some Christians might be careful about how much they evangelise because they might be worried about people being offended or even persecuting them for their faith. They might find other ways to spread the word of God, like living a life according to Biblical teachings which sets an example for others.
   [4 marks available — see p.75 for mark scheme]
5 Spreads the word of God abroad *[1 mark]*
6 - Reconciliation means making peace between people. Jesus said, "Blessed are the peacemakers" (Matthew 5:9 NIV), so Christians believe that they should work to promote peace in the world in order to be blessed.
   - Some Christians believe that they have a duty to make peace in the world. Peter writes that people "must seek peace and pursue it" (1 Peter 3:11 NIV).
   - Christians believe that people are all equal, and part of one community, so we should try to live in harmony together and promote peace. In Colossians 3:15 it says "Let the peace of Christ rule in your hearts, since as members of one body you were called to peace" (NIV).
   - Jesus was a peaceful man, so in order to follow his example and lead a Christian life, Christians should promote peace across the world. Jesus taught that if someone slaps you on one cheek, you should "turn to them the other cheek also" (Matthew 5:39 NIV).
   [5 marks available — see p.75 for mark scheme]
7 Arguments that support the statement:
   - The most important duty of a local church is to look after its congregation. Peter describes the congregation as "God's flock that is under your care" (1 Peter 5:2 NIV) and instructs church leaders to watch over them.
   - Jesus said "For where two or three gather in my name, there am I with them" (Matthew 18:20 NIV). This means that to develop a relationship with Jesus, worshipping as a community is the most important thing.
   - Many Christians across the world still experience terrible persecution for their faith. It is the responsibility of churches to provide spiritual comfort, and ideally physical safety, to Christians in danger within their community.
   - Spreading the word of God to more people is vital. Jesus sent out his disciples to "preach the gospel to all creation" (Mark 16:15 NIV), so creating a Christian community through evangelism is the most important role of Christian churches.

Arguments against the statement:
- Jesus gathered disciples (pupils) and spent much of his ministry teaching them, and others, about God and his kingdom. Christians try to follow the example of Jesus as he was the Son of God, so the most important role of the church is to teach about God and his kingdom.
- The most important role of the church is to be a place for services of worship. Churches also perform important ceremonies like marriages, funerals and baptisms which are hugely important milestones in the lives of Christians. These services and ceremonies are largely the same across the world, and have been largely the same for centuries. This means that they continue the traditions of the Church, and help people feel part of a global community.
- Jesus was sympathetic to the poor and taught that the most important commandment was to "Love your neighbour as yourself" (Mark 12:31 NIV). As a result, many Christians believe that the most important work of the Church is supporting charity work in the local area, for example youth groups or food banks.
[12 marks available — see p.75 for mark scheme]

Beliefs, Teachings and Practices — Islam
Pages 17-18 — Key Beliefs in Islam
1. Beneficent *[1 mark]*
2. Malaikah *[1 mark]*
3. - Belief that Allah is the one and only god (Tawhid)
   - Belief in angels (Malaikah)
   - Belief in the holy books (Kutub)
   - Belief in Allah's prophets (Nubuwwah)
   - Belief in the day of judgement (Yawm ad-Din)
   - Belief in predestination (al-Qadr)
   [2 marks available, 1 mark for each correct point]
4. - Muslims will not accept that there may be more than one god. To do so would be shirk, which is considered to be the gravest of all sins. For example, Muslims disagree with the Christian concept of the Holy Trinity, as it goes against Tawhid.
   - Muslims will affirm this belief through the shahadah. Many Muslims repeat this belief through shahadah several times throughout the day, as well as at key events such as birth, deaths and marriages.
   - Muslims will avoid making images of Allah as this risks shirk. Worshipping images and statues is similar to the forbidden worship of idols. Instead, Islamic art has found other ways of representing Allah visually, e.g. through depicting some, or all, of the ninety-nine names of Allah.
   - When explaining Islam to non-Muslims, Muslims may tell them about Tawhid.
   [4 marks available — see p.75 for mark scheme]
5. Shirk *[1 mark]*
6. - God is one, undivided and the only god, without equal: "Say, O Prophet, 'He is God — One and Indivisible' " (Qur'an 112:1).
   - God is merciful and kind and forgives people of their sins. The majority of chapters in the Qur'an begin with the assertion Allah is merciful (the bismillah): "In the name of God — the Most Compassionate, Most Merciful" (Qur'an 1:1).
   - God is all powerful (omnipotent). He created all things and is in control of all things. This includes people and their actions (predestination).
   - God is infinitely good (beneficent) and just. Allah wishes people to live well and revealed how to do this to the prophets. He judges people fairly, rewarding the good and punishing the evil.
   - God is present in the world (immanent) and yet above it and unfathomable to human beings (transcendent). Allah takes a personal interest in the lives of all people yet is without equal in the whole of existence: "Indeed it is We Who created humankind and fully know what their souls whisper to them, and We are closer to them than their jugular vein" (Qur'an 50:16).
   - God has many characteristics, indicated by the ninety-nine names of Allah. These ninety-nine names originate in the Qur'an and describe a combination of what God is, what he has done, what he can do and what he will do — e.g. Al-Khaaliq (the creator).
   [5 marks available — see p.75 for mark scheme]

7. Arguments that support the statement:
   - The two groups hold different beliefs about who succeeded the caliph Ali. After the death of Ali in 661 CE the two groups separated.
   - Sunni Muslims believe no person after Muhammad received knowledge from Allah. In contrast, Shi'a Muslims believe, as an article of faith, that the imams receive knowledge from Allah and so possess special authority (Imamate).
   - Sunni Muslims hold six articles of faith, while Shi'a Muslims hold five articles of faith. Whilst there is some overlap (e.g. Tawhid, Nubuwwah) there are key differences (e.g. Imamate).
   - Sunni Muslims adhere to the Five Pillars, while Shi'a Muslims adhere to the Ten Obligatory Acts.
   - There are key differences in practices including how and when the five prayers are said each day (salah). Sunni Muslims pray at five points during the day, Shi'a Muslims at three points. Sunni Muslims will touch their heads to the ground for each rak'ah, while Shi'a Muslims touch their heads to something natural, such as wood or clay. Both Sunni and Shi'a Muslims practise giving to charity (Zakah), however Shi'a Muslims also pay khums as an additional tax on 20% of their excess wealth each year.
   - Sunni and Shi'a Muslims interpret and mark Ashura differently. Sunni Muslims interpret the festival as marking the day of atonement when minor sins can be forgiven through fasting. Shi'a Muslims believe the festival marks the death of Husayn and represent this through dressing in black, holding processions and performing passion plays.
   Arguments against the statement:
   - The two groups fundamentally agree in most beliefs about Allah. The oneness of God (Tawhid) is a central belief of both Sunnis and Shi'as, as is the belief that shirk is the chief sin.
   - There is substantial overlap between the two sets of articles of faith, particularly in the oneness of God (Tawhid), prophethood (Nubuwwah) and a day of judgement (Yawm al-Din).
   - Both Sunni and Shi'a Muslims agree on ideas that Allah predestines all things and in the existence of angels. Whilst Shi'a Muslims may not hold them as articles of faith, they are still important beliefs.
   - Muhammad and his ethical teachings (Hadith) are central to all Muslims, as are the broader teachings and practices of Muhammad (Sunnah). They are important for interpreting the Qur'an and living according to Allah's will.
   - All Muslims agree that the beliefs which come from the Qur'an are the unaltered teachings of Allah. As such, this commonly accepted holy text unifies all Muslims.
   [12 marks available — see p.75 for mark scheme]

Pages 19-20 — Authority
1. Ibrahim *[1 mark]*
2. Imamate *[1 mark]*
3. - Imams are all descended from Muhammad.
   - Imams have divine knowledge.
   - Imams are infallible, incapable of being wrong.
   - The largest group of Shi'a Muslims, Twelvers, believe there have been 11 imams, and a twelfth will appear at the end of time.
   - Nizari Muslims believe there is an unbroken line to the current imam, the Aga Kahn.
   [2 marks available, 1 mark for each correct point]
4. - The Qur'an guides Muslims. It tells them everything they need to know about Allah and how to lead their lives according to his wishes. Muslims try to live according to the instructions given in the Qur'an — for example, in what they eat, when, where and how they pray and giving to charity.
   - Some Muslims may choose to learn the Qur'an by heart as they believe it is an exact record of Allah's words to Muhammad.
   - Muslims may choose to live, and resolve disagreements and issues, according to the guidance of the shari'ah law contained in the Qur'an.
   [4 marks available — see p.75 for mark scheme]

5. Surah *[1 mark]*
6. - There are four holy books aside from the Qur'an: the Tawrat (Torah), the Suhuf (scrolls of Ibrahim), the Zabur (Psalms) and the Injil (Gospels). All holy books are equally important, but none of the books apart from the Qur'an contain the perfectly recorded teachings of Allah.
   - The scrolls of Ibrahim are the earliest of the holy books but have been lost: "This is certainly mentioned in the earlier Scriptures — the Scriptures of Abraham and Moses" (Qur'an 87:18-19). It is believed that Ibrahim received a number of teachings from Allah.
   - The Tawrat was the holy book given to the prophet Musa. It is the main Jewish holy book but is valued by Muslims as it contains "God's judgement" (Qur'an 5:43).
   - The Injil was given to Isa (Jesus). Muslims believe the Christian gospels contain the main ideas given to Isa, but are imperfect as they were written down from what his followers remembered after Isa ascended into heaven: "We sent Our messengers, and after them We sent Jesus... and granted him the Gospel" (Qur'an 57:27).
   - The Zabur was given to the prophet Dawud (David). However, like the Tawrat and Injil, Muslims believe the Zabur as written in the Christian Bible and Jewish Tenakh are corrupted, with the original Zabur lost forever: "We revealed the Torah, containing guidance and light" (Qur'an 5:44) / "...to David We gave the Psalms" (Qur'an 4:163).
   [5 marks available — see p.75 for mark scheme]
7. Arguments that support the statement:
   - In the first revelation, Muhammad was commanded by the angel Jibril to read out what would become Surah 96. Receiving the revelations that would become the Qur'an took the next twenty-three years of Muhammad's life. The task was not completed quickly, but continued over time, suggesting it was his main role.
   - The teaching of messengership (risalah) explains that the role of a prophet is to receive the message of Allah through angels. The Qur'an identifies 25 prophets who have taken on this role, including Muhammad. As such, messengership could be seen as his primary role.
   - Muhammad was Allah's final prophet (the 'seal of the prophets') with no more to follow. His life centred around receiving and reciting the Qur'an, and ensuring his scribes recorded the teachings, suggesting this role took precedence over all others.
   Arguments against the statement:
   - Muhammad's main role was to be a model for how to live according to Allah's wishes. Preaching the Qur'an was one aspect of this role, but living in accordance to Allah's wishes was Muhammad's main role, as it is for all Muslims.
   - Muhammad's role cannot be reduced to just a single element. It included preaching and recording what was revealed to him as well as exemplifying these teachings and becoming a spiritual and political leader in Makkah.
   - Muhammad played an important role in the spread and preservation of Islam. He helped to establish Islam across the Arab world and acted to defend both the Islamic faith and Muslim communities from hostile forces.
   [12 marks available — see p.75 for mark scheme]

Page 21 — Life after Death

1. al-Akhirah *[1 mark]*
2. Paradise *[1 mark]*
3. - The angel Israfil will sound the trumpet.
   - The Earth will be destroyed.
   - The living will die.
   - The dead will be resurrected.
   - Allah will judge all people according to their deeds.
   - Those judged to have lived good lives will go to paradise, those judged to have lived immoral lives will go to hell.
   [2 marks available, 1 mark for each correct point]
4. Arguments that support the statement:
   - Predestination (al-Qadr) is an important teaching in Islam. It is stated repeatedly that a person cannot do other than what Allah has chosen for them. This belief is incompatible with human freedom as they logically contradict each other.
   - Holding the belief of predestination is not compatible with free will as it can lead to people rejecting their own free will and responsibility to make good choices. This is illustrated by the Hadith in which a man asks whether he should tie up his camel so it doesn't walk off or whether he should leave it untied and have faith that Allah will ensure that the camel will remain there: "'Shall I tie it and rely (upon Allah), or leave it loose and rely (upon Allah)?' He said: 'Tie it and rely (upon Allah)'" (Jami' at-Tirmidhi 2517). This demonstrates that people must be responsible for their own actions and so must have free will.
   Arguments against the statement:
   - It must be possible to believe in these two ideas as the purpose of this life is to achieve an afterlife in paradise through good thoughts and deeds. This means not just doing the actions Allah has determined, but going about them with the right intention.
   - Sunni Muslims typically believe that while Allah determines an individual's choices, they come into ownership of the choice when they consciously make it themselves.
   - While everything that happens is predetermined by Allah, humans are in control of their own reactions and responses to events. Being outside of time, Allah knows in advance what these choices will be, and has planned the world accordingly.
   [12 marks available — see p.75 for mark scheme]

Page 22 — Worship

1. Wudu *[1 mark]*
2. - Sunni Muslims will give five sets of prayers at five separate points during the day. Prayer will be given at dawn, after midday, in the late afternoon, at sunset and at night.
   - Some Sunni Muslims may combine sets of prayers if they have a good reason that prevents them from praying five times a day, e.g. when travelling.
   - In contrast, Shi'a Muslims give five sets of prayers but often combine them into three points during the day, combining midday with afternoon prayers and sunset with night time prayers.
   - Sunni Muslims typically carry out each rak'ah on a prayer mat and touch their foreheads directly onto the mat or the ground. When standing, they will cross their hands.
   - Shi'a Muslims typically touch their heads to something natural (wood or clay) during each rak'ah and do not cross their hands when standing.
   - During Friday prayers, men are often expected to pray at a nearby mosque.
   - However, women will typically pray where they normally would throughout the week.
   [4 marks available — see p.75 for mark scheme]
3. - Shahadah is the first of the Five Pillars of Islam. While all the pillars are equally important, Shahadah has a special place as the central pillar, as without this one the others would not be possible.
   - It is the Muslim declaration of faith. The declaration is not directly from a holy book but comes from key passages in the Qur'an: "God Himself is a Witness that there is no god worthy of worship except Him" (Qur'an 3:18).
   - It is said repeatedly throughout the day, for instance in the call to prayer (adhan). It is also said at important points during a Muslim's life, such as birth, death or when a person converts to Islam.
   - For many Shi'a Muslims, it is important that the declaration includes reference to Ali: "Ali is the helper of Allah" — therefore the Shahadah is also important in showing Shi'a belief in Ali.
   [5 marks available — see p.75 for mark scheme]

Pages 23-24 — Duties

1. Ihram *[1 mark]*
2. Laylat al-Qadr *[1 mark]*
3. The Ka'aba and/or the black stone, Zamzam Well, Safa and/or Marwa, Mount Arafat, Muzdalifa, the three pillars at Mina.
   [2 marks available, 1 mark for each correct point]
4. - Charity (zakah) is one of the Five Pillars for Sunni Muslims and one of the 10 Obligatory Acts for Shi'a Muslims. It involves giving away 2.5% of a person's wealth each year to charitable causes.

- For Shi'a Muslims, charity may refer to Khums, another of the Ten Obligatory Acts. It is a 20% tax on all surplus earnings and wealth for the purposes of Islamic education and helping those in need.
[4 marks available — see p.75 for mark scheme]

5 Struggle *[1 mark]*

6 - Sawm symbolises physical and spiritual discipline in obedience to Allah. It encompasses more than simply fasting, but abstaining from sexual relations, wasting time and harmful actions.
- It is required by the Qur'an: "O believers! Fasting is prescribed for you — as it was for those before you — so perhaps you will become mindful of God" (Qur'an 2:183).
- For Sunni Muslims, sawm is one of the Five Pillars. For Shi'a Muslims, it is one of the Ten Obligatory Acts.
- It is an expression of thanksgiving for the Qur'an, which is believed to have first been given to Muhammad on the Night of Power: "Indeed, it is We Who sent this Qur'an down on the Night of Glory" (Qur'an 97:1) / "The Night of Glory is better than a thousand months" (Qur'an 97:3). Many Muslims will read the Qur'an from start to finish while fasting during Ramadan to mark this key point in Muslim history.
- It is a reminder for Muslims to prioritise spirituality and religious responsibilities. The annual demands of sawm act to aid Muslims in re-aligning their lives to the will of Allah:
"...Whoever fasts during the month of Ramadan out of sincere faith and hoping to attain Allah's rewards, then all his past sins will be forgiven" (Sahih al-Bukhari Volume 1, Book 2, Hadith 37).
[5 marks available — see p.75 for mark scheme]

7 Arguments that support the statement:
- Jihad represents the internal struggle of every Muslim to live according to Allah's teachings and be a good Muslim. As such, it may be argued that it encompasses a person trying to fulfil the whole range of duties required in Islam.
- The 'greater jihad' is personal and individual. Ultimately, each person will be held to account for their own thoughts and deeds, and jihad is the duty to live accordingly.
- For Shi'a Muslims, jihad is one of the Ten Obligatory Acts.
- Another interpretation of jihad is as the struggle to make the world a better place. This is a broader, higher duty than that which one owes oneself. It is rooted in care and compassion for others. This selflessness was exemplified in the life of Muhammad.
Arguments against the statement:
- While jihad is one of the Ten Obligatory Acts for Shi'a Muslims, no one duty is held to be more important than the others. Jihad is not one of the Five Pillars for Sunni Muslims, and so arguably should not be considered one of the main duties of a Muslim's life.
- It could be argued that Shahadah is the central duty. While none of the duties are more important than the others, Shahadah is the pre-requisite for the others.
- Salah is a very important duty as it brings a person in close contact with Allah. It is the chief discipline to avoid believing in other gods (shirk) which is the worst sin.
- Jihad can refer to physical struggle or conflict. While violence is sometimes necessary, in self-defence or defence of another for instance, it is not the overriding duty of a person's life.
- Jihad has been used by extremist groups to justify aggressive actions against innocents. The vast majority of Muslims condemn this interpretation of jihad and so would not view this interpretation as a duty.
[12 marks available — see p.75 for mark scheme]

Page 25 — Festivals

1 Ibrahim *[1 mark]*

2 - For Shi'a Muslims, the festival marks an occasion of sorrow and this is reflected in how they mark it. As the festival commemorates the death of Husayn, Shi'a Muslims may wear black as a sign of mourning. They may take part in processions and passion plays depicting the death of Husayn.
- Some Shi'a Muslims harm themselves to share in the experience of Husayn's suffering. This practice is controversial within Shi'a Islam and has been banned in some countries.
- Some Sunni Muslims will fast during Ashura, as they view it as a day of atonement, but it is not compulsory to do so.
- Sunni Muslims discourage the harming of the body to mark Ashura. This practice is believed to conflict with teachings about preserving and respecting the body.
[4 marks available — see p.75 for mark scheme]

3 - The festival marks the end of the holy month of Ramadan. It celebrates strength in the face of adversity after a month of fasting: "O believers! Fasting is prescribed for you — as it was for those before you — so perhaps you will become mindful of God" (Qur'an 2:183).
- It is a festival of spiritual renewal. Many Muslims feel closer to Allah after completing the fourth pillar, sawm, and have spent time refocusing on their spiritual life: "And to fast is better for you, if only you knew" (Qur'an 2:184).
- It marks the point by which charity for that month (Zakah ul-Fitr) must be given. For many Muslims, the importance of compassion and charity is a focus during the previous month of fasting.
- The festival was celebrated by Muhammad himself from 624 CE. Muslims believe Muhammad lived perfectly according to Allah's will, which suggests it is right to celebrate Id-ul-Fitr.
[5 marks available — see p.75 for mark scheme]

Theme A — Relationships and Families

Page 26 — Sexuality and Sexual Relationships

1 Promiscuity *[1 mark]*

2 Viewpoints that oppose homosexuality:
- The book of Leviticus states: "If a man has sexual relations with a man as one does with a woman, both of them have done what is detestable" (Leviticus 20:13 NIV). Some Christians use this to argue that homosexuality is wrong.
- Some Muslims believe homosexual relationships are forbidden by Islam due to teachings in the Qur'an, such as the story of Sodom and Gomorrah.
Viewpoints that support homosexuality:
- Jesus taught about equality and stood up for people in the minority. Some Christians therefore see everyone as being equal, regardless of sexuality.
- The Qur'an only forbids homosexual actions, not feelings, so it doesn't condemn actually being homosexual.
[4 marks available — see p.75 for mark scheme]

3 - The Catholic Church teaches that one of the main reasons for marriage is to "be fruitful and increase in number" (NIV), as instructed by God in Genesis 9:7. They think artificial contraception is wrong because it goes against this teaching, and prevents life, which is a gift from God.
- Some Christians think family planning is important as it enables couples to only have children when they're ready.
- In Islam, any form of contraception has to be 'reversible', because Muslims should aim to have children at some point within their marriage. Therefore, sterilisation and vasectomies are not permitted.
- Muslims don't agree with any forms of contraception that they would see as causing an abortion, e.g. the morning after pill. Muslims believe that life is sacred and the Qur'an states that "whoever takes a life... it will be as if they killed all of humanity" (Qur'an 5:32).
[5 marks available — see p.75 for mark scheme]

Pages 27-28 — Marriage and Divorce

1 Divorce *[1 mark]*

2 - The Catholic Church holds the view that homosexual acts are wrong and that marriage should be between a man and a woman, so opposes same-sex marriage.
- Some Church of England clergy believe we are all accepted by God and will say prayers for a same-sex couple following a civil (non-religious) marriage ceremony. In 2023, the Church of England General Synod voted in favour of trialling same-sex marriage blessing services.

- Many Muslims are against same-sex marriage based on teachings from the Qur'an, which say homosexual sex is forbidden.
- Some Muslims believe that being homosexual is normal and therefore same-sex couples should have the chance to marry.

[2 marks available, 1 mark for each correct point]

3 - Roman Catholics believe that divorce is impossible due to marriage being a sacrament.
- Some Christians, such as many from the Church of England, believe people should be given second chances and so should be allowed to divorce.
- In Islam, divorce is permitted but has to be requested on three separate occasions over a three month period.
- According to Muslims, Allah does not take divorce lightly.

[2 marks available, 1 mark for each correct point]

4 Viewpoints that support cohabitation:
- Some people believe that cohabitation is perfectly acceptable in preparation for marriage, or as an alternative to it.
- Pope Francis recognised that it can be hard for people to marry, because it costs a lot of money, but also said they should be encouraged to marry eventually.
Viewpoints that oppose cohabitation:
- Some traditional Christians believe that sex outside marriage is wrong and they therefore reject cohabitation.
- Many Muslims reject the idea of living together because they believe that sex outside marriage is a sin.

[4 marks available — see p.75 for mark scheme]

5 Adultery *[1 mark]*

6 - Christians teach that marriage was part of God's intention when he created Eve as a "suitable helper" for Adam (Genesis 2:20-22 NIV). The purpose of marriage is for companionship.
- Christians view marriage as very important as it creates a strong union between the couple, which reflects the union between Christ and the Church. Marriage partners show this commitment to one another when they make their vows.
- Muslims believe that it is Allah's will for couples to be married as it clearly states in the Qur'an: "Marry off the free singles among you" (Qur'an 24:32). The purpose is to provide love, stability and companionship.
- Muslims believe that marriage is very important because it provides the right environment for having children. Families are a key feature in Islamic culture and marriage is viewed as an essential part of developing the faith.

[5 marks available — see p.75 for mark scheme]

7 Arguments that support the statement:
- Roman Catholics do not think divorce is possible and therefore neither is remarriage. They believe marriage to be permanent because it is a sacrament: "Therefore what God has joined together, let no-one separate" (Mark 10:9 NIV).
- Marriage ceremonies involve making a commitment by exchanging vows and rings. Some people hold the view that this commitment is permanent and you are married 'for life', so a second marriage would not be acceptable.
- Some people believe that divorce and remarriage are damaging to children. Remarriage can sometimes create problems for stepchildren and step-parents when trying to form relationships with one another.
Arguments against the statement:
- Protestants believe that Jesus's teaching on marriage and divorce in the New Testament shows the ideal way to which all Christians should aspire. They accept, however, that sometimes humans fall short of this ideal and make mistakes, so therefore they need to be given a second chance.
- The Church of England accepts that sometimes marriages fail and that people need to have second chances. They use Jesus's teachings about forgiveness to support their views (e.g. the story of the woman who had committed adultery in John 8:2-11). People can remarry in a Church of England church if the minister agrees to do the ceremony.
- In Islam, after a divorce, both men and women are considered to be free to re-marry, so remarriage is acceptable.

- For some divorced people, remarrying may help them to form a happy, stable household, providing a positive environment for children to grow up in.

[12 marks available — see p.75 for mark scheme]

Page 29 — Families

1 Nuclear *[1 mark]*

2 Viewpoints that support same-sex parenting:
- In the UK, same-sex couples can adopt, foster and legally use a surrogate to create a family. Therefore, some people completely support same-sex parenting.
- Some believers hold the view that the most important aspects of a family are security and love. They consider these values to be more important than the sexual orientation of the parents and accept that the most loving thing is to adapt religious teachings to the modern world.
- Some less traditional believers think that an individual's happiness is at the heart of a relationship. They therefore support same-sex parenting as long as the couple are in a loving relationship.
Viewpoints that oppose same-sex parenting:
- Some traditional believers hold the view that heterosexual relationships provide the role models children need to grow and develop within a family. They see this as being part of God's plan. They argue that same-sex parenting cannot provide the same role models.
- The Roman Catholic Church teaches that same-sex parenting is wrong. This is due to their beliefs that God created men and women to form a family, and due to their rejection of homosexuality.
- Most Muslims do not support the idea of same-sex parenting because they believe homosexuality is wrong.

[4 marks available — see p.75 for mark scheme]

3 - Many Christians believe that children are a gift from God, and that parents have a responsibility to teach them to live how God would want them to: "bring them up in the training and instruction of the Lord" (Ephesians 6:4 NIV).
- Christian parents might teach their children key passages from the Bible such as the 10 Commandments or The Lord's Prayer. Parents are encouraged to do this in the Old Testament: "These commandments that I give you today are to be on your hearts. Impress them on your children." (Deuteronomy 6:6-7 NIV).
- Muslim parents believe that educating their children about Islam is a crucial part of their role: "This was the advice of Abraham — as well as Jacob — to his children, saying, 'Indeed, God has chosen for you this faith; so do not die except in a state of full submission'" (Qur'an 2:132).
- Rituals such as the naming ceremony (aqiqah) and the bismillah ceremony (where a child first starts to learn about Islam) are considered crucial in ensuring Muslim children have clear understanding of their faith.

[5 marks available — see p.75 for mark scheme]

Page 30 — Gender Equality

1 Gender inequality *[1 mark]*

2 Shared parental leave *[1 mark]*

3 - Roman Catholic and Orthodox churches won't allow women to be priests, so these denominations believe men and women can be treated differently.
- Anglican churches now allow women to be bishops, indicating that they are equal to men.
- Some Muslims believe that man was created first and therefore has authority over women.
- Many Muslims interpret the Qur'an as saying that men and women have different roles within the community, but do have equal status.

[2 marks available, 1 mark for each correct point]

4 Arguments that support the statement:
- Most modern Christians do not believe that men are superior to women. They use Paul's teachings in Galatians 3:28 which says "nor is there male and female, for you are all one in Christ Jesus" (NIV) to support their views.

- Many modern Christians point to the creation story Genesis 1:27: "So God created mankind in his own image, in the image of God he created them; male and female he created them" (NIV). This implies men and women are equal.
- In Islam, the woman is traditionally the homemaker whilst the man is the breadwinner. It can be argued that this doesn't indicate that one gender has higher status than the other — the roles are simply different.
- Shared parental leave was introduced in the UK in 2015 and promotes the idea that parents can share the time taken off work during the first year of their child's life.

Arguments against the statement:
- Some Christians interpret Genesis as evidence that men are superior to women because God makes a woman out of the rib of Adam to be his helper.
- Some Christians look to St Paul's teachings for evidence that the man is meant to be the head of the family. For example, "Wives, submit yourselves to your own husbands..." (Ephesians 5:22 NIV).
- The Church of England still allows the option in the vows for the woman to "love, honour and obey" her husband. Therefore, some traditional Christian families are patriarchal, viewing the husband as the 'head of the household'.
- Some teachings in the Qur'an may imply that men are superior to women: "Men are the caretakers of women" (Qur'an 4:34). This could imply that women have to be obedient to men.
- Paid maternity leave is much longer than paid paternity leave. This might suggest that society views women as being the main carer for children and men as the breadwinner.
[12 marks available — see p.75 for mark scheme]

Theme B — Religion and Life
Pages 31-32 — The Universe and the Environment
1 The Big Bang theory *[1 mark]*
2 Dominion *[1 mark]*
3 - The universe was created by God.
   - The universe was created in six days.
   - After creating the universe, God rested for a day.
   - The universe was created according to the Big Bang theory but controlled by God.
   - The creation story in the book of Genesis is a metaphor for how God created the universe.
   [2 marks available, 1 mark for each correct point]
4 - Christians believe that God gave humans the Earth to look after. This is known as stewardship. They believe that all Christians have a duty to take care of the environment.
   - Muslims believe that humans are khalifah (trustees or vice-regents) of the world. This means that they have a duty to act as stewards and to protect the environment.
   [4 marks available — see p.75 for mark scheme]
5 Only human life is sacred *[1 mark]*.
6 - Christians believe the Biblical creation story in Genesis, which says that God "created mankind in his own image" (Genesis 1:27 NIV). This means that humans are special, and should respect each other.
   - Christians believe that man was created "from the dust of the ground" (Genesis 2:7 NIV) and woman "from the rib he had taken out of the man" (Genesis 2:22 NIV). This shows the care and attention that God paid to creating humans, which suggested that humans are more important to God than animals.
   - The Qur'an says that Allah created humans "from clay" (Qur'an 32:7). The first man was Adam, and Allah breathed life and a soul into him. This shows that human life is sacred because it comes from Allah.
   - Many religious people believe in the theory of evolution — that humans evolved from animals. They see the creation story as a metaphor for this — God created humans and animals using the process of evolution.
   [5 marks available — see p.75 for mark scheme]

7 Arguments that support the statement:
   - Many Christians believe that animals should be treated with kindness. The Bible says that "The righteous care for the needs of their animals" (Proverbs 12:10 NIV), so experimenting on animals is wrong.
   - Christians believe that God created the world, so it is special. They have a responsibility to take care of it — this is known as stewardship. Some argue that experimenting on animals goes against this principle, so is wrong.
   - Muslims believe that the Earth is a product of Allah's love, so they should treat it with love and respect. They are khalifah of the Earth (similar to stewardship) so they must protect it. Some Muslims argue that this means animal experimentation is wrong because it causes suffering to the animals that we should be protecting.
   Arguments against the statement:
   - Utilitarians believe the right thing to do is the one that brings about the most good. Some utilitarians believe that experimenting on animals can be right if it will lead to a lot of people being helped or many lives being saved.
   - Catholicism teaches that experiments on animals can be acceptable, but only if they will benefit mankind. The Catechism of the Catholic Church says that experimentation on animals "is a morally acceptable practice if it remains within reasonable limits and contributes to caring for or saving human lives" (Catechism 2417-2418). Humans must not make animals suffer or die without good reason.
   - Some Muslims argue that human life is so valuable that in special cases, animal experimentation is not wrong. However, even in these cases, the animals must be treated humanely and they should not suffer any unnecessary pain.
   [12 marks available — see p.75 for mark scheme]

Pages 33-34 — Abortion and Euthanasia
1 When a pregnancy is deliberately ended without the birth of a living child *[1 mark]*.
2 The patient's quality of life is so bad that death is more compassionate *[1 mark]*.
3 - Before 24 weeks if continuing to be pregnant would be worse for the mother's physical and mental health (if two doctors agree).
   - At any time if the mother's life is at serious risk.
   - At any time if the foetus has a serious disability.
   [2 marks available, 1 mark for each correct point]
4 Viewpoints that believe the sanctity of life is the most important factor:
   - Some Christians believe abortion is undesirable since God "created mankind in his own image" (Genesis 1:27 NIV), so even unborn babies are the images of God.
   - The Catholic Church strongly believes that all life is sacred, and therefore humans cannot end it deliberately. Most Catholics are against abortion and euthanasia for this reason. The Catechism of the Catholic Church describes euthanasia as "murder" (Catechism 2277).
   - Muslims believe that life is sacred because Allah has a plan for all humans and only he can decide when humans die: "No soul can ever die without God's Will at the destined time" (Qur'an 3:145).
   Viewpoints that believe other factors need to be considered:
   - Some Christians believe that allowing a woman to choose whether she has an abortion or not is a way of showing Christian compassion.
   - Atheists and humanists believe that we should weigh the sanctity of life against quality of life. For example, they might believe that abortion should be allowed if the quality of life of the baby once it's born will be very low.
   [4 marks available — see p.75 for mark scheme]
5 Belgium *[1 mark]*

6   - Catholic Christians believe euthanasia is always wrong. They believe that life is so sacred that it is a form of murder even to withdraw treatment from someone. The Catechism of the Catholic Church says "an act or omission which... causes death in order to eliminate suffering constitutes a murder" (Catechism 2277).
- Some Anglican Christians believe that they must have compassion for people when they are suffering, especially when their quality of life is poor. Treatment can be withdrawn from patients who are dying in very painful ways, or who have incurable illnesses.
- Many Muslims believe that euthanasia is wrong because life belongs to Allah and only he can decide when human lives end. They also believe that suffering is a test that people need to go through — "...who say, when struck by a disaster, 'Surely to God we belong and to Him we will all return' " (Qur'an 2:156).
[5 marks available — see p.75 for mark scheme]

7   Arguments that support the statement:
- Muslims believe that after 120 days of pregnancy, the soul enters the foetus (ensoulment) — "the soul is breathed into his body" (Sahih al-Bukhari 55:549). This leads some Muslims to believe that before this time abortion can be allowed in some circumstances, for example if the baby would be born with a serious disability.
- Some Christians (for example the Church of England) argue that abortion should be allowed in certain situations such as when the mother's life is at risk. They believe that the situation should be approached with Christian compassion.
- Many humanists believe that abortion is undesirable, but that it should be the choice of the mother. They argue that women should be able to decide what happens to their bodies.
Arguments that disagree with the statement:
- The Qur'an teaches that killing is wrong, so some Muslims believe that abortion is always wrong as it involves ending a human life. The Qur'an says "Do not kill your children... killing them is a heinous sin" (Qur'an 17:31).
- Christians believe God created humans "in his own image" (Genesis 1:27 NIV), and some argue this makes abortion wrong.
- Roman Catholic Christians believe that human life begins at conception, so all abortion is a form of murder. The Catechism of the Catholic Church says, "The deliberate murder of an innocent person is gravely contrary to the dignity of the human being... and to the holiness of the Creator" (Catechism 2261).
[12 marks available — see p.75 for mark scheme]

Page 35 — The Afterlife

1   Believing in the afterlife is a comfort to people when someone dies *[1 mark]*
2   Reincarnation *[1 mark]*
3   - There isn't any evidence of a life after death, so there is no reason to believe in it.
- Memories of previous lives could be false, so they do not count as evidence.
- Stories about ghosts can often be explained by people being mistaken, so there is not enough evidence to believe that they are people who are living after death.
- Much of the evidence for the afterlife comes from religious teachings, but if you do not believe in that religion, there is no reason to believe in the afterlife.
[2 marks available, 1 mark for each correct point]
4   Arguments that support the statement:
- Muslims believe that after death they will either go to paradise (jannah) or hell (jahannam). Their ultimate aim is to spend eternity in jannah in the afterlife, so it could be argued that it must be more important than life on Earth.
- A key part of the Christian faith is that Jesus was resurrected from death, and returned to heaven at the ascension to prepare a place there for those that believe in him. The afterlife is therefore central to Christianity, and ultimately joining Jesus in heaven is more important than any experience on Earth.
Arguments against the statement:
- According to Islam, the afterlife for the righteous will be like paradise — the word for heaven, 'jannah', actually means garden. However, to get there Muslims must lead a righteous life, so life on Earth is extremely important.
- Most Christians believe that they should aim to bring about the kingdom of God. Many Christians believe that the afterlife is extremely important because that is where the kingdom will come to be. However, some Christians believe that the kingdom can exist on Earth. Jesus said that "the kingdom of God is in your midst" (Luke 17:21 NIV). This means that life on Earth could be just as important as the afterlife.
- Non-religious people might not believe in an afterlife, so they would say that life on Earth is all that matters. Others might argue that even if an afterlife exists, we have little to no evidence of what it will actually be like. For this reason, it makes sense to live as if there is no afterlife, and focus only on life on Earth.
[12 marks available — see p.75 for mark scheme]

Theme C — The Existence of God and Revelation

Page 36 — Design and Causation

1   Charles Darwin *[1 mark]*
2   A watch *[1 mark]*
3   - Complicated things like the human eye seem to have been designed.
- The argument is supported by the Qur'an and the Bible.
- The universe itself is very complicated, so people argue it could not have come about by chance.
- It is compatible with science — evolution could be the way God designed his creation.
[2 marks available, 1 mark for each correct point]
4   Arguments that support the statement:
- The First Cause argument fits with Islamic and Christian sacred texts, which describe the universe being created by God. God is the First Cause who makes the rest of creation happen.
- Christianity teaches that God is "eternal" (Deuteronomy 33:27 NIV) and "everlasting" (Isaiah 40:28 NIV). This means he would have existed before the universe, so he could be the First Cause.
- It could be argued that the Big Bang theory supports the statement. God could have caused the Big Bang and therefore been the First Cause of the universe.
Arguments against the statement:
- Even if we accept that there is a First Cause, this is not necessarily proof that God exists. The First Cause could be a different kind of being or thing. The argument certainly does not prove the existence of the kind of God described in Christian and Muslim holy books and teachings.
- Some people argue that the First Cause argument doesn't make sense. If everything needs to have a cause, they argue, why doesn't the First Cause also need to be caused by something?
[12 marks available — see p.75 for mark scheme]

Pages 37-39 — Miracles and Revelation

1   Separate from the world *[1 mark]*
2   Visions *[1 mark]*
3   - The feeding of the 5000 in the Bible.
- Jesus turning water into wine.
- The Qur'an itself.
[2 marks available, 1 mark for each correct point]
4   - Religious experiences are private, so it is impossible to prove to another person that they happened.
- People who claim to have had a religious experience might actually have a mental health issue or a condition of the brain that makes them believe they have seen something that isn't really there.
- Believers might choose to interpret their experience in a religious way whereas a non-religious person might interpret it in a different way.
[2 marks available, 1 mark for each correct point]
5   They were written centuries ago *[1 mark]*
6   - Christians believe that nature can show God's existence by demonstrating his qualities. For example, Catholics believe that "The beauty of creation reflects the infinite beauty of the Creator" (Catechism of the Catholic Church 341). Some believe the cruelty of nature came after the Fall, and so this does not reflect the nature of God.

Answers

- Muslims believe that people can be convinced that Allah exists by looking at nature. Nature's beauty demonstrates the qualities of Allah, such as beauty. One of the 99 names of Allah, Al-Musawwir (The Shaper of Beauty), demonstrates this.
[5 marks available — see p.75 for mark scheme]

7   Viewpoints that believe in revelation:
- Nature is considered a form of general revelation. Christians believe that the beauty of nature reveals the wonder and intelligence of God himself.
Viewpoints that do not believe in revelation:
- Some Christians believe that nature can be cruel, so it no longer reveals God's true nature.
- Atheists believe that the world can be explained by science, even if we have not discovered it yet. This means that there is no reason to see nature as a revelation from God.
[4 marks available — see p.75 for mark scheme]

8   - Muslims believe that the Qur'an was directly revealed to Muhammad. It contains the exact words of Allah as revealed to Muhammad, and this is the final revelation from Allah to humans. The Qur'an says, "Then God revealed to His servant what He revealed through Gabriel. The Prophet's heart did not doubt what he saw" (Qur'an 53:10-11).
- Many Christians believe that the Bible was written by humans, but inspired by God: "All Scripture is God-breathed" (2 Timothy 3:16 NIV). It contains his message, but it needs to be interpreted by humans.
[5 marks available — see p.75 for mark scheme]

9   - Many Muslims believe that the prophets performed miracles. This showed their power, and the fact that they had been sent by God.
- Many Christians believe that Jesus performed miracles in the Gospels. These miracles showed Jesus's power, and that he was the Son of God.
[4 marks available — see p.75 for mark scheme]

10 Arguments that support the statement:
- Visions are direct and powerful — they can often convince the person who experienced them that God exists, as this seems to be the only explanation for what they have been through.
- Many visions occur in scripture, and they often predict things that then happened. For example, in the Qur'an, the angel Jibril appeared to Maryam to tell her she was going to have a son, which she then did. The large number of stories of visions throughout history convinces people that God must exist for so many people to have had direct experiences of him.
- Some visions completely change the lives and beliefs of even people who don't believe in God. In the Bible, Saul persecuted Christians, but one day he saw a vision of Jesus. He completely changed his life as a result, and dedicated his life to God. Some Christians argue that if a vision could change someone's mind so completely, it must show that God exists.
Arguments against the statement:
- Visions might be powerful to those who experience them, but they are almost always personal. No one else can experience the same thing, so they might only convince one person that God exists.
- Sufi Muslims claim to experience visions and other direct experiences of Allah. However, some other Muslims are sceptical of these claims, and do not believe these experiences are real. If even people from the same religion are sceptical of claims, they cannot be used to prove that Allah exists.
[12 marks available — see p.75 for mark scheme]

Page 40 — Arguments Against the Existence of God
1   Atheist *[1 mark]*
2   There isn't enough scientific evidence that they happened *[1 mark]*.
3   - Many scientists believe that there is no need to explain the creation of the universe using a God. They believe that the Big Bang theory gives enough of an explanation that a God isn't needed.
- The theory of evolution can be used to explain how life and human beings came to be. There is no need for a creator God to form animals and humans.
- Science is based on the collection of physical evidence to test a hypothesis. Many scientists argue that, since God is claimed to be a supernatural being, there is just not enough physical evidence to show God exists, so it must then be concluded that he does not exist.
[2 marks available, 1 mark for each correct point]

4   - Christians believe that God gave humans free will to choose to do good or evil. St Augustine argued that the price to pay for free will was the suffering that sometimes happened as a result.
- Muslims believe that suffering is part of Allah's plan, even if we do not understand it. We must trust that Allah has this plan, and tolerate the suffering that is part of it.
- Some people argue that suffering is a punishment for sin. As a result of Adam and Eve disobeying God, all humans carry 'original sin'. Suffering is punishment for this and other sins committed in the believer's life.
- Atheists and humanists might argue that evil and suffering can't be punishments for sin, because they are experienced by almost everyone. Also, animals suffer as well, and it doesn't make sense to say that these animals are being punished for sinning.
[4 marks available — see p.75 for mark scheme]

Theme D — Religion, Peace and Conflict
Pages 41-42 — Peace and Conflict
1   Violent protest *[1 mark]*
2   Forgiveness *[1 mark]*
3   - It must be started by a proper authority, e.g. government or head of state.
- There must a good reason, e.g. self-defence or protection of others/innocents.
- All alternatives to conflict or war must have been attempted.
- The war must have a reasonable chance of success.
- The harm caused must be proportionate to the harm or evil the war is trying to prevent.
[2 marks available, 1 mark for each correct point]

4   - Terrorism contradicts one of the key Christian principles, the belief that they should treat others as they would wish to be treated, so it is never acceptable to harm innocents to further a cause.
- Christians see passive resistance as a better way to achieve change or further a cause. For example, this can be seen in the efforts of Dr Martin Luther King who did not resort to violence.
- Terrorism goes against the peaceful principles of Islam — the Qur'an instructs Muslims to reply peacefully when they are addressed harshly.
- Muslims believe peaceful protest or passive resistance are the best ways to fight injustice — this was demonstrated by many Muslims in the 2011 Arab Spring.
- While Islamic terrorists have sometimes used the term 'jihad' to justify their actions, the overwhelming majority of Muslims view this as wrong, because terrorism involves harming innocent people.
[4 marks available — see p.75 for mark scheme]

5   Holy War *[1 mark]*
6   - Christians believe that reconciliation is extremely important, as Jesus died on the cross in order to reconcile human beings with God. Just as God forgives people and is reconciled with them, Christianity teaches the importance of reconciliation between people themselves: "Blessed are the merciful, for they will be shown mercy" (Matthew 5:7 NIV).
- Many Christians believe it is important to help groups or individuals in conflict reconcile their differences. For example, Archbishop Desmond Tutu led the Truth and Reconciliation Commission after apartheid ended in South Africa.
- Muslims believe that Allah is merciful and so it is possible for those who sin to be reconciled with Him.
- In Islam, working towards reconciliation between groups in conflict is encouraged. Muslims follow this teaching: "And if two groups of believers fight each other, then make peace between them" (Qur'an 49:9).
[5 marks available — see p.75 for mark scheme]

7   Arguments that support the statement:
    - Some religious believers would support the pacifist ideals that the use of violence can never be justified by religion or any other reason.
    - The Bible teaches Christians to be peaceful: "all who draw the sword will die by the sword" (Matthew 26:52 NIV).
    - Islam teaches that peace is to be preferred over violence: "The true servants of the Most Compassionate are those who walk on the earth humbly, and when the foolish address them improperly, they only respond with peace" (Qur'an 25:63).
    - Some believers may argue that while violence may be justified on some grounds, it should never be carried out for religious reasons. Many now reject the idea of Holy War and do not believe that a just war can have a religious justification.
    For example, some Muslims believe that war is only justified in self-defence, or to protect other Muslims or Muslim countries.
    - Some believers may argue that religious justification can't be used where the violence is indiscriminate or targets innocents. So the use of weapons of mass destruction or terrorism are not allowable, even if a conflict is otherwise justified by religion.
    Arguments against the statement:
    - Some religious believers may argue that religious principles involve defending the weak and vulnerable, and that this can sometimes involve violence. They may believe that, while non-violent opposition to injustice is preferable, it is sometimes necessary to resort to violence in order to preserve justice. Jesus seemed to condone some acts of violence for religious reasons when he threw the money lenders from the temple (Matthew 21:12).
    - Some believers may refer to religious principles which dictate when and how violence should be used. Often this is with a view to bringing about peace through violent means when such a path is unavoidable. Violence can be justified on religious grounds within the concept of the lesser jihad: "So fight them and God will punish them at your hands, put them to shame, help you overcome them..." (Qur'an 9:14). Military jihad, however, is subject to very strict rules with many similarities to the Just War theory.
    - Traditionally, the concept of Holy War has been used to justify violence on religious grounds. Religious teachings on just war are found in the writings of St Augustine and St Thomas Aquinas, and are reflected in contemporary Christian teachings such as the Catechism of the Catholic Church (2265).
    [12 marks available — see p.75 for mark scheme]

Page 43 — Weapons of Mass Destruction
1   Indiscriminate *[1 mark]*
2   Viewpoints in favour of possessing nuclear weapons:
    - Some Christians and Muslims believe that the possession of nuclear weapons is justified in order to preserve peace. The principle of mutually assured destruction means that just having nuclear weapons can be enough to stop countries starting a war.
    Viewpoints against possessing nuclear weapons:
    - Some believe that the possession of nuclear weapons is completely at odds with many Christian teachings. It is wrong to possess weapons which, by their nature, are intended to cause the indiscriminate death of soldiers and civilians alike.
    - Most Islamic countries do not agree with possessing nuclear weapons because of their destructive and indiscriminate nature. Where military defence is necessary, as governed under the rules of the lesser jihad, it is preferable to possess conventional military weapons which can be directed more specifically.
    [4 marks available — see p.75 for mark scheme]
3   - The use of weapons which may indiscriminately harm civilians, land and animals alike goes against Christian principles of peace and respect for God's creation: "When you lay siege to a city for a long time... do not destroy its trees by putting an axe to them, because you can eat their fruit" (Deuteronomy 20:19 NIV).
    - Jesus taught his followers to "love your enemies" (Luke 6:27 NIV), which many Christians believe prohibits the use of weapons of mass destruction. Similarly, they should not be used as a form of retaliation if others use them: "If anyone slaps you on your right cheek, turn to them the other cheek also" (Matthew 5:39 NIV).
    - The use of weapons of mass destruction that involves the killing of innocents would be considered murder in Islam and so is prohibited: "...whoever takes a life... it will be as if they killed all of humanity" (Qur'an 5:32).
    - Muslims believe that even if the use of violence could be justified, it is likely that weapons of mass destruction fall outside of the rules of jihad because they are indiscriminate: "Do not kill women or children or an aged, infirm person. Do not cut down fruit-bearing trees. Do not destroy an inhabited place" (Hadith Muwatta Malik 21:10).
    [5 marks available — see p.75 for mark scheme]

Page 44 — Peacemaking
1   Retaliation *[1 mark]*
2   Campaign for Nuclear Disarmament *[1 mark]*
3   - By raising money where they live.
    - By providing essentials such as food and medical supplies to be delivered by other organisations.
    - By campaigning and putting pressure on governments and international organisations to intervene.
    - By acting as mediators between groups in conflict with one another.
    - By organising or attending protests against conflicts.
    [2 marks available, 1 mark for each correct point]
4   Arguments that support the statement:
    - Some religious believers may argue that each person's first responsibility is to build and preserve their relationship with God. No person is without sin and so individuals ought to focus on their own actions before becoming involved in the conflicts of others.
    - Many Muslims believe that the struggle to obey Allah and become a better Muslim (greater jihad) is given priority over the struggle to make the world a better place (lesser jihad): "No soul burdened with sin will bear the burden of another" (Qur'an 35:18).
    - Some Christians may argue that while making peace with others is to be encouraged, developing their faith is the most important thing, as it is through that they'll receive God's grace. They believe that salvation comes through belief in Jesus as saviour: "I am the resurrection and the life. The one who believes in me will live, even though they die" (John 11:25 NIV).
    Arguments against the statement:
    - Many religious believers would argue that peace is always to be preferred over violence. There are many religious teachings which consistently identify peace, reconciliation and forgiveness as central features of God's creation.
    - For Christians, those who seek peace and try to help others achieve peace are identified positively by Jesus in the Sermon on the Mount: "Blessed are the peacemakers, for they will be called children of God" (Matthew 5:9 NIV).
    - Many religious leaders, such as Archbishop Desmond Tutu, were successful in resolving conflicts between others. By following their example and working towards the same goal it could be said that people may also be building their own relationship with God.
    - Muslims may follow the example of the Prophet Muhammad who worked to restore peace between others: "Good and evil cannot be equal. Respond to evil with what is best, then the one you are in a feud with will be like a close friend" (Qur'an 41:34).
    - Atheists and non-religious people may argue that there is no higher goal than working towards a peaceful world. They may believe that it is wrong to focus on oneself over helping others.
    [12 marks available — see p.75 for mark scheme]

Theme E — Religion, Crime and Punishment
Pages 45-46 — Law, Crime and Forgiveness
1   Poverty *[1 mark]*
2   Sin *[1 mark]*
3   Murder, theft, robbery, assault, fraud, rape
    [2 marks available, 1 mark for each correct point]
4   - Christianity teaches that God is forgiving and that people should be forgiving too. This is demonstrated in many teachings and practices, from the Lord's Prayer to the Catholic sacrament of reconciliation.

- Christianity teaches that forgiveness depends on repentance. This means that forgiveness can only happen when a person is truly sorry and wishes to be forgiven.
- Islam teaches that it is always better to be forgiving than to seek retribution. The Prophet Muhammad exemplifies this in the Hadith and many Muslims aim to follow his example.
- Muslims believe that there are some sins which are so bad they cannot be forgiven. For example, the sin of believing in multiple gods (shirk).
[4 marks available — see p.75 for mark scheme]

5 Intention *[1 mark]*

6 - Christians believe that people should obey God's law as well as obeying the laws of the state they are in: "Then Jesus said to them, 'Give back to Caesar what is Caesar's and to God what is God's.' And they were amazed at him" (Mark 12:17 NIV).
- Christians believe that where the laws of the state conflict with God's law, people should obey God's law first: "We must obey God rather than human beings!" (Acts 5:29 NIV).
- Muslims believe that God's law should be obeyed. The law, which is called shari'ah, is contained in the Qur'an and other teachings: "God commands justice, grace, as well as generosity to close relatives. He forbids indecency, wickedness, and aggression" (Qur'an 16:90). Many Muslim countries base the state law on the shari'ah law.
- Muslims believe that breaking God's law will result in punishment on the Day of Judgement, if criminals do not seek forgiveness from God: "He admits whoever He wills into His mercy. As for the wrongdoers, He has prepared for them a painful punishment" (Qur'an 76:31).
[5 marks available — see p.75 for mark scheme]

7 Arguments that support the statement:
- People have free will and so if they choose to abuse free will by committing crime, the responsibility rests with the individual themselves. Both religious believers and non-religious people may agree with this if they accept that human beings are capable of making their own choices.
- Part of what makes crimes bad is the intention behind the criminal action. If a person chooses to break the law and understands what they are doing, they alone should bear responsibility for this.
- In the parable of the sheep and the goats, Jesus taught that people will be judged by God on their actions and how they treated others in life. They are held to account for their actions, and so are responsible for any crimes they may have committed.
- Muslims believe that each person's deeds and intentions are recorded by angels, and that Allah will judge each person on how they spent their time on Earth. So they are held responsible for their own actions, including crimes.
- For Muslims, this hadith on intention means that if a crime was intended then a person will be judged on that intention: "The reward of deeds depends upon the intentions and every person will get the reward according to what he has intended" (Hadith Sahih al-Bukhari 1:1).
Arguments against the statement:
- There are some reasons why a person may not be responsible for a crime they committed. For example if a person commits a crime because of mental illness, most people would not regard this as their fault.
- Sometimes, responsibility for crime might be placed with society. For example, many people believe that poverty, addiction and a troubled upbringing can all contribute to the likelihood that a person will commit crime. While this might not excuse criminal activities entirely, the failure of society to deal with these problems could be seen as a mitigating factor.
- Muslims acknowledge that many factors can contribute to criminal activity, including poverty and addiction, and may give zakah to charities which reduce the effects of these factors.
- Some people believe that, when faced with an unjust law, a person has no choice but to break it in order to stick to a higher moral law or God's law. Responsibility for crime may lie with the law itself. Many Christians have consciously defied unjust laws where they conflicted with God's law, for example Rosa Parks and Dr Martin Luther King.
[12 marks available — see p.75 for mark scheme]

Pages 47-48 — Punishment and the Death Penalty

1 Utility *[1 mark]*
2 Human Rights *[1 mark]*
3 - Punishment is an important way to preserve justice.
- Punishment gives criminals a chance to reform.
- Punishment can provide rehabilitation for criminals.
- Punishment can be justified as a deterrent to others.
- Punishment can be used to protect the public from dangerous individuals.
- Punishment can be used to compensate the victim or victims of crime.
[2 marks available, 1 mark for each correct point]

4 Viewpoints that are in favour of the death penalty:
- Some Christians may be in favour of the death penalty, as they believe it protects the innocent against further crimes. They may use teachings in the Old Testament (e.g. demanding bloodshed in payment for bloodshed, or putting to death anyone who kills someone with a blow) to justify this belief.
- Muhammad outlined three areas that were subject to the death penalty: murder, adultery and abandoning Islam. Some Muslims therefore believe that the death penalty may be justified in certain cases.
Viewpoints that oppose the death penalty:
- Many Christians oppose the death penalty as it does not show mercy or allow for the criminal to be reformed or rehabilitated. The Sermon on the Mount places an emphasis on loving one's enemy, even where this is very difficult.
- Some Muslims view the ending of life as an area reserved for Allah, who is able to act with perfect judgment, knowledge and authority. Because of this, they do not agree with the use of the death penalty. Also, Muhammad encouraged families of victims to take compensation from the criminal instead of going through with the death penalty.
[4 marks available — see p.75 for mark scheme]

5 Mentor *[1 mark]*
6 - Some Christians believe that corporal punishment should be avoided, as it involves the use of violence. Even when used as a punishment, it is still violence being used against other human beings: "all who draw the sword will die by the sword" (Matthew 26:52 NIV).
- Some Christians might argue that there could be circumstances where corporal punishment can serve a purpose. The Bible, especially Old Testament, contains many references to corporal punishment: "If the guilty person deserves to be beaten, the judge shall... have them flogged... with the number of lashes the crime deserves" (Deuteronomy 25:2 NIV).
- Corporal punishment is permitted under Islamic law (shari'ah) as way of punishing serious crimes. These crimes can include stealing, adultery and drinking alcohol: "As for... thieves, cut off their hands for what they have done — a deterrent from God" (Qur'an 5:38).
- However, some Muslims believe that these punishments are too severe, and they're not used by all Muslim communities. Those who do agree with corporal punishment believe it should only be carried out under very strict conditions. For example, where there are multiple witnesses to a crime to ensure that there is no doubt about the criminal's guilt.
[5 marks available — see p.75 for mark scheme]

7 Arguments that support the statement:
- Prison should be a form of retributive punishment for criminal wrongdoing. If it is a positive experience, it undermines this idea — if a criminal enjoys their punishment then it's not really a punishment.
- The Qur'an states that the punishment should fit the crime "...an eye for an eye" (Qur'an 5:45), and so some Muslims believe that criminals who have committed terrible crimes should have an unpleasant experience in prison.
- For Christians, teachings in the Old Testament reinforce the idea that crime requires punishment: "Whoever does not obey the law of your God and the law of the king must surely be punished by... imprisonment" (Ezra 7:26 NIV).

- Some people believe that if prison was a positive experience, it would not act as a deterrent to other criminals. They might argue that prison should be, and should be seen as, an unpleasant punishment for people who have inflicted suffering on others. This will then discourage other potential criminals from committing crimes.
- Similarly, in relation to rehabilitation, prisons can only reform criminals if they understand that there are negative consequences to committing crimes. If prison is a positive experience, it could undermine the effectiveness of prisons in discouraging criminals from re-offending after they are released.

Arguments against the statement:
- Prison is a punishment as it deprives criminals of their freedom, so they're still being punished just by being in prison.
- Christians look to the parable of the sheep and the goats, in which Jesus blesses those who show compassion towards prisoners: "Truly I tell you, whatever you did for one of the least of these brothers and sisters of mine, you did for me" (Matthew 25:40 NIV). The experience of being in prison should be made positive in order to demonstrate this compassion.
- The Qur'an is also clear that prisoners are vulnerable members of society and should be treated fairly and with compassion: "and give food — despite their desire for it — to the poor, the orphan, and the captive" (Qur'an 76:8).
- The main aims of prisons should be to protect society, punish criminals and reform them. Keeping prisoners locked up achieves the first two and making prison a more positive experience makes reformation more effective in the long run by promoting rehabilitation.

[12 marks available — see p.75 for mark scheme]

Theme F — Religion, Human Rights and Social Justice

Pages 49-50 — Attitudes to Equality

1 Sexism *[1 mark]*
2 The Equality Act *[1 mark]*
3 Any two from: age, sex/gender, disability, gender reassignment, marriage and civil partnership, pregnancy/maternity, race, religion or belief, sexual orientation.
[2 marks available, 1 mark for each correct point]
4 Points that show support of gender equality:
- Many Protestant Christians have female ministers and leaders, recognising equal status of gender.
- The expectations of all Muslims regarding key religious duties is the same regardless of gender. For example, the Five Pillars of Islam are expected to be adhered to by all Sunni Muslims.
Points that suggest a lack of gender inequality:
- Roman Catholic Christians hold the view that men and women have very specific roles within Church. Only men are able to be members of the clergy.
- Men are expected to attend the mosque in Islam, whereas for women it is optional. If both genders attend, then women and men are separated for worship.
[4 marks available — see p.75 for mark scheme]
5 Positive discrimination *[1 mark]*
6 - Christianity teaches that there should be no discrimination on grounds of race. St Paul said: "There is neither Jew nor Gentile... for you are all one in Christ Jesus" (Galatians 3:28 NIV).
- The first chapter of Genesis says that "God created mankind in his own image" (Genesis 1:27 NIV), which suggests that all people are a likeness of God, regardless of race.
- Muslims follow the teaching in the final sermon of Muhammad, which makes it clear that racism is wrong. He said "Between Muslims there are no races and no tribes".
[5 marks available — see p.75 for mark scheme]

7 Arguments that support the statement:
- Jesus said to "Love your neighbour as yourself" (Mark 12:31 NIV), meaning that everyone should be treated as you would expect to be treated yourself. So it could be argued that Christians have been instructed to work for equality.
- The Bible teaches that humans all come from God: "God created mankind in his own image" (Genesis 1:27 NIV). This makes it clear that all humans should be treated with respect, so believers should aim to achieve equality.
- In Islam, the principle of the Muslim community, the ummah, sets an example of equality. All Muslims (regardless of race, gender or age) are seen as one united community. There are different types of Muslims, such as Shi'a and Sunni, but these are all part of the universal principle of ummah. This principle suggests that Muslims should support equality.

Arguments against the statement:
- Leadership on equality doesn't only come from religion. The Equality Act of 2010 was set up to promote the view that everyone is equal. This means it is against the law for anybody to treat others unequally. It could be argued that government should lead the way on equality.
- Although some of St Paul's writings preach equality, 1 Corinthians 6:9-10 forbids homosexuality, and 1 Timothy 2:12 says women shouldn't teach or have authority over a man. So the message from the Bible isn't always one of equality, and some Christians may not believe in working for equality in all areas.
- Some Muslims believe that whilst equality is important due to the ummah, certain conditions may mean that individuals do not have to be treated equally. For example, some Muslims reject homosexuality, so may not believe in working for full equality in the area of sexual orientation.

[12 marks available — see p.75 for mark scheme]

Page 51 — Human Rights and Freedom of Belief

1 The United Nations *[1 mark]*
2 Conversion *[1 mark]*
3 - The Catholic Church teaches that every individual has a responsibility to ensure that human rights are protected.
- The Qur'an says "God commands justice, grace, as well as generosity" (Qur'an 16:90), so Muslims think justice and human rights are very important.
[2 marks available, 1 mark for each correct point]
4 Arguments that support the statement:
- Many Christians would support people's right to choose their own beliefs. The Catechism of the Catholic Church 174 says "The right to the exercise of freedom, especially in religious and moral matters, is an inalienable requirement of the dignity of man."
- The Qur'an says "Let there be no compulsion in religion" (Qur'an 2:256), so most Muslims feel people should be allowed to choose whether to follow Islam.
- It could be argued that everyone should be allowed to make up their own mind about their beliefs, without pressure from believers speaking to them forcefully, e.g. in schools or on the street.

Arguments against the statement:
- Jesus said: "I am the way and the truth and the life. No-one comes to the Father except through me" (John 14:6 NIV). Some Christians therefore believe that non-Christians need to be converted to Christianity to be saved, so do not encourage freedom of religion.
- In Islam, many believe that converting away from Islam or becoming an atheist (apostasy) is a terrible sin. So freedom of religion might not be seen as possible in Islam.
- Some might argue that people shouldn't have the right to express religious beliefs that discriminate against others, such as criticism of homosexual relationships. They might therefore feel that complete religious freedom should not be allowed.

[12 marks available — see p.75 for mark scheme]

Pages 52-53 — Social Justice, Wealth and Poverty

1. Everyone should be treated fairly *[1 mark]*.
2. Amnesty International *[1 mark]*
3. Unemployment, lack of skills, lack of fair pay, high living costs, war, exploitation
   [2 marks available, 1 mark for each correct point]
4. - Christians view human trafficking as slavery and believe that they have a duty to prevent it happening. The Bible tells people to support and speak up for those who are poor and can't protect themselves.
   - Islam prohibits human trafficking. The Qur'an says that people who set slaves free are righteous, and condemns anyone who forces women into prostitution.
   - The Global Freedom Network has been created collectively by Catholic, Anglican and Sunni Islam leaders. The aim of this is to eradicate people trafficking on an international level.
   [4 marks available — see p.75 for mark scheme]
5. National living wage *[1 mark]*
6. - The story of the widow's offering (Mark 12:41-44) suggests that people have a duty to give as much to the poor as they can afford. It is not the amount they give that matters, but the fact that they are being generous with what they have.
   - Christians should have a positive attitude to giving to the poor: "God loves a cheerful giver" (2 Corinthians 9:7 NIV).
   - One of the Five Pillars of Islam (zakah) states that Muslims should give 2.5% of their wealth each year to those in need.
   - In the hadith, Muslims are instructed to help those in poverty: "A man is not a believer who fills his stomach while his neighbour is hungry" (Al-Adab al-Mufrad 6:112).
   [5 marks available — see p.75 for mark scheme]
7. Arguments that support the statement:
   - In Christian teaching, it is the love of money, rather than money itself, which is condemned. 1 Timothy 6:10 says, "the love of money is a root of all kinds of evil" (NIV). Those with wealth should be willing to give their money away to help others.
   - Islamic teaching focuses on the idea that money is a gift from Allah and therefore it should be used to help others. This is demonstrated in the work of Muslim charities such as Islamic Aid and Muslim Aid.
   - Some people might argue that it is their right to receive money and use it how they wish if they have worked hard. Money isn't evil if it is their just reward for their work.
   Arguments against the statement:
   - In the Sermon on the Mount, Jesus says, "You cannot serve both God and Money" (Matthew 6:24 NIV). This might suggest that possession of money is intrinsically opposed to living as God would like one to do.
   - Jesus said, "It is easier for a camel to go through the eye of a needle than for someone who is rich to enter the kingdom of God" (Mark 10:25 NIV). This suggests that even if someone is generous with their wealth, they are going against God's ways if they possess lots of money, and so money must be evil.
   - Islam says people shouldn't use money to make a profit from others. The Qur'an states: "God has... forbidden interest" (Qur'an 2:275). It is also seen as wrong to make money from alcohol or sex. So certain ways of making and using money are seen as evil.
   [12 marks available — see p.75 for mark scheme]

Theme G — St Mark's Gospel: the Life of Jesus
Page 54 — The Start of Jesus's Ministry

1. John *[1 mark]*
2. He sent angels to look after him *[1 mark]*
3. - It links Jesus to Old Testament prophesies about the Messiah.
   - It means 'anointed one', which shows how special Jesus is.
   - The title 'Messiah' was given to kings of Israel, which shows how important Jesus is.
   - The Messiah was supposed to save the Jews from their enemies.
   [2 marks available, 1 mark for each correct point]
4. Arguments that support the statement:
   - Mark's Gospel doesn't contain any information about Jesus's birth. It begins with John the Baptist and Jesus's baptism. This suggests that this story is important because it is the beginning of Jesus's ministry — the beginning of the 'good news' that Mark wanted to tell in the Gospel.
   - The appearance of the Holy Spirit in the form of a dove, and the sound of the voice of God, shows that Jesus is the Son of God. Jesus's identity as the Son of God is central to Christianity, so the story where this is first declared could be seen as the most important.
   - The story is the most important because Christians are still baptised today. Their baptism marks them joining the church and becoming Christians, following in the footsteps of Jesus.
   Arguments against the statement:
   - The story of Jesus's death and resurrection is the most important. It is through this that the sins of mankind are forgiven, which means that Christians can go to heaven.
   - The parables of Jesus are the most important stories in Mark's Gospel. They tell Christians what the kingdom of God will be like, which is the basis of the Christian faith.
   - The story of Jesus's baptism isn't the most important because it only marks the beginning of Jesus's teachings. Christians use the gospels as guides to show them how to act. The baptism only tells them they should be baptised. It is the rest of the gospel which shows them what to do to follow Jesus's example.
   [12 marks available — see p.75 for mark scheme]

Page 55 — Jesus's Miracles

1. His daughter *[1 mark]*
2. - Some Christians believe that the miracle stories are literally true. Jesus broke the laws of nature, showing his power, which must have come from God.
   - Others believe that the miracle stories are just metaphors which teach spiritual truths, and shouldn't be taken literally.
   - Some atheists believe that the miracles didn't happen at all — the events can be explained by science or the events didn't happen as they were described.
   [4 marks available — see p.75 for mark scheme]
3. - The paralysed man's friends couldn't get him inside the house because the crowd was too large. They carried him onto the roof and made a hole to lower him down. This shows their determination, and suggests to Christians that if they have faith in Jesus and show determination, they will be rewarded.
   - Jesus said to the man, "Son, your sins are forgiven" (Mark 2:5 NIV). It is only after some teachers of the law began to question his ability to forgive sins that he showed his power by healing the man's paralysis. This shows that, to Jesus, forgiving sins is more important than healing the body.
   - When the teachers of the law questioned how Jesus could forgive sins, Jesus replied that "the Son of Man has authority on earth to forgive sins" (Mark 2:10 NIV). For Christians, this is evidence that Jesus was the Son of God.
   [5 marks available — see p.75 for mark scheme]

Pages 56-57 — The Later Ministry of Jesus

1. Moses *[1 mark]*
2. On a donkey *[1 mark]*
3. - He would be delivered to the chief priests and teachers of the law.
   - He would be condemned to death.
   - He would be handed over to the Gentiles/Romans.
   - He would be mocked/spat at/flogged.
   - He would be killed, but he would rise again after three days.
   [2 marks available, 1 mark for each correct point]
4. - Some Christians believe Jesus entered Jerusalem in glory — he was greeted by large crowds. They shouted greetings at him, saying "Blessed is he who comes in the name of the Lord!" (Mark 11:9 NIV).
   - In contrast, some Christians believe Jesus entered Jerusalem in humility. He rode a donkey rather than a horse, and instead of a carpet he walked on leaves and cloaks.

- Some Christians believe Jesus was celebrated by the crowd as the Messiah — they shouted "Blessed is the coming kingdom of our father David!" (Mark 11:10 NIV). Jesus was the saviour that had been predicted in the Old Testament.
- In contrast, some Christians believe instead of the military leader people expected for their Messiah, Jesus entered on a donkey peacefully. This shows that he was not going to be a military leader, as predicted in the Old Testament.
[4 marks available — see p.75 for mark scheme]

5 - Jesus's clothes became a dazzling white.
- Elijah and Moses appeared and spoke to Jesus.
- A cloud appeared to cover them.
- God spoke to the disciples.
[2 marks available, 1 mark for each correct point]

6 - James and John both wanted to sit in important places to the left and right of Jesus, but Jesus told them that to be first, they must "be slave of all" (Mark 10:44 NIV). This teaches Christians to be humble and to put others before themselves.
- This story shows Christians that Jesus is humble, and wished to serve mankind rather than be a military or political leader. He said he "did not come to be served, but to serve" (Mark 10:45 NIV). This leads Christians to worship Jesus, and to try to follow his example.
- Jesus predicts that James and John "will drink the cup I drink" (Mark 10:39 NIV). This means that they will have to suffer persecution in a similar way to Jesus. This is important to Christians because when they are suffering, they can feel less alone as Jesus understands what they are going through, and Christians in the past have also experienced the same suffering.
[5 marks available — see p.75 for mark scheme]

7 Arguments that support the statement:
- Jesus tried to hide his miracles. For example, he told Jairus not to spread the news about Jesus bringing his daughter back to life. Bringing someone back from the dead would be seen as proof that Jesus was the Messiah, so the fact that he tried to hide it shows that Jesus did not see himself as the Messiah.
- Jesus does not refer to himself as the Messiah. Instead he calls himself the Son of Man, which some people suggest was just a simple way of talking about himself. It would have been easy for him to call himself the Messiah, especially in front of trusted disciples. The fact that he didn't shows it is not how he saw himself.
- The Messiah whose coming is predicted in the Old Testament is a military leader who "will deliver us from the Assyrians when they invade our land and march across our borders" (Micah 5:6 NIV). Jesus knew he was not this military leader, so he tried to stop people from calling him the Messiah.
Arguments against the statement:
- Jesus drew huge crowds, which could make things very difficult for him and others. For example, the friends of the paralysed man had to lower him through the roof to avoid the crowd. Jesus saw himself as the Messiah, but it made practical sense for him to try and stop news of his miracles from spreading.
- Some Christians believe that Jesus tried to hide his messiahship for as long as possible because he knew he would quickly be arrested for it, as it would be seen as blasphemy. He wanted more time to spread the word about the kingdom of God.
- Although Jesus saw himself as the Messiah, he might have avoided that title to try to prevent his followers getting the wrong idea about his mission. When Jesus told the disciples that he would be killed, Peter "began to rebuke him" (Mark 8:32 NIV). Peter may have believed in the Messiah as a military leader who would defeat the authorities rather than be killed by them.
- Jesus does refer to himself as the Son of Man. Some people believe that this was just a normal way of referring to oneself at the time, but the Son of Man is written about in Daniel. There he is described as having authority and power, and having a kingdom which "will never be destroyed" (Daniel 7:14 NIV).
[12 marks available — see p.75 for mark scheme]

Pages 58-59 — The Final Days in Jerusalem

1 It was Passover *[1 mark]*
2 Bethany *[1 mark]*
3 - They drank wine.
- They broke bread and ate it.
- Jesus predicted that one of the disciples would betray him.
- Jesus said that the bread is his body and the wine is his blood.
- Jesus predicted his own death.
[2 marks available, 1 mark for each correct point]

4 - Some Christians believe that Jesus's crucifixion was the only way that human beings could be forgiven for their sins and therefore get to heaven.
- In contrast, some Christians believe that Jesus's death wasn't necessary for God to forgive humanity. A God who is loving, merciful and omnipotent should be able to forgive people's sins anyway.
- Some Christians believe that Jesus's crucifixion is important because it shows how much God loves human beings — he gave his only son to save us.
- In contrast, some Christians believe that the crucifixion was important because it led to the resurrection, which shows that God is so powerful that he can triumph over death.
[4 marks available — see p.75 for mark scheme]

5 The temple curtain ripped *[1 mark]*
6 - While praying in the Garden of Gethsemane, Jesus asks God to "Take this cup from me" (Mark 14:36 NIV). This brief weakness shows Jesus's humanity, and helps Christians who are suffering to remember that Jesus also suffered.
- Jesus submits to God's will, saying "Yet not what I will, but what you will" (Mark 14:36 NIV). This teaches Christians that no matter what they are going through, they must trust in God's will.
- Judas betrayed Jesus with a kiss, and then Jesus was arrested. This teaches Christians that they might be persecuted during their lives.
- The disciples fell asleep instead of watching for Jesus. They also ran away after Jesus was arrested. He says "The spirit is willing, but the flesh is weak" (Mark 14:38 NIV). This shows that even those who have the strongest faith sometimes lose it or fail. Christians must always try to keep faith, even when they face strong temptations.
[5 marks available — see p.75 for mark scheme]

7 Arguments that support the statement:
- Jesus predicted his death many times in Mark's Gospel, for example at Caesarea Philippi. If he had wanted to avoid being arrested, he could have stopped teaching, or travelled somewhere else to teach. He did not, so he chose to accept his own death.
- It is important that Jesus chose to die for the sins of humanity. He had no sins himself, but loved humanity so much that he sacrificed himself to save us. If Jesus had not deliberately chosen to die, humanity would not have been saved.
- Jesus knew that one of his disciples would betray him. At the last supper he told them all that "one of you will betray me" (Mark 14:18 NIV). He could have named Judas and had him sent away to stop the betrayal, but he chose to let Judas organise his arrest.
Arguments against the statement:
- It is clear that Jesus wanted to hide the fact that he was the Son of God and the Messiah. For example, he told Jairus not to tell anyone that he had brought his daughter back from the dead. Some people argue that this is because he did not want to be arrested and killed.
- In the Garden of Gethsemane, Jesus first asks that his suffering be removed, and then submits to God's will, saying "Yet not what I will, but what you will" (Mark 14:36 NIV). This shows that Jesus knows he must be killed because it is the will of God.
- Jesus's death fulfilled prophecies from the Old Testament. Jesus had no choice but to let himself be arrested, saying "the Scriptures must be fulfilled" (Mark 14:49 NIV).
[12 marks available — see p.75 for mark scheme]

Answers

Theme H — St Mark's Gospel as a Source of Spiritual Truths

Pages 60-61 — The Kingdom of God

1. It was written by an anonymous author *[1 mark]*.
2. A teacher of the law *[1 mark]*
3. - At first it will be very small.
   - It will grow to be very large.
   - It will include non-Jews (the birds) as well as Jews.
   [2 marks available, 1 mark for each correct point]
4. Viewpoints that show children were valued:
   - People brought their children to Jesus because they wanted him to bless them. This shows that they cared about their children greatly.
   - Jesus was angry with the disciples for sending away the children. He took the time to bless them, showing that he valued children.
   - Jesus loved young children and said that the kingdom of God belonged to them.
   Viewpoints that show children were not valued:
   - The disciples were angry with the people who brought their children. This suggests that they didn't think children were important enough to take up Jesus's time.
   [4 marks available — see p.75 for mark scheme]
5. - Some fell on the path and were eaten by birds.
   - Some fell on thin, rocky soil. They grew quickly and then withered in the sun.
   - Some fell among thorns and were choked as they grew.
   - Some fell on good soil, grew well and produced a good crop.
   [2 marks available, 1 mark for each correct point]
6. - Jesus told the rich man to "give to the poor" (Mark 10:21 NIV), which leads many modern day Christians to give to charity and volunteer for causes which help the poor.
   - Jesus told the rich man to "sell everything you have" (Mark 10:21 NIV). Some modern Christians like nuns or monks believe that this means they should try to live completely without wealth or personal possessions.
   - Jesus told the rich man that it is "easier for a camel to go through the eye of a needle than for someone who is rich to enter the kingdom of God" (Mark 10:25 NIV). Some Christians believe that Jesus's comparison of a rich man and a camel passing through the eye of a needle means that they can still own possessions, but that money should not be their main focus in life.
   - Some modern Christians see this story as important because it shows Jesus as a humble leader. He was happy to remain poor and didn't need wealth or possessions. This makes him worthy of their worship.
   [5 marks available — see p.75 for mark scheme]
7. Arguments that support the statement:
   - In the parable of the mustard seed, Jesus described the kingdom of God growing from a small seed. Christians interpret this to mean that his teachings are the small seed, which will then spread amongst the disciples and across the earth, making a physical kingdom.
   - Some Christians argue that the kingdom is already partially here, because Jesus showed God's power over nature, sin and death through the miracles of Jesus. Although it is partly here as a physical location, it has not fully arrived yet.
   - At the last supper, Jesus said that he would not drink wine again "until that day when I drink it new in the kingdom of God" (Mark 14:25 NIV). This suggests that the kingdom of God will be a physical place where Jesus will be in the future.
   - The Lord's prayer (in Matthew and Luke) says "your kingdom come, your will be done, on earth as it is in heaven" (Matthew 6:10 NIV). This suggests that the kingdom of God will, at some point, be a real place on earth.
   Arguments against the statement:
   - When Jesus blessed the young children, he said that "anyone who will not receive the kingdom of God like a little child will never enter it" (Mark 10:15 NIV). Here he seems to imply that people can receive the kingdom into their hearts today. This suggests that the kingdom is a state of being rather than a physical place.
   - When the teacher of the law agreed with Jesus about the greatest commandment, Jesus replied "You are not far from the kingdom of God" (Mark 12:34 NIV). The teacher of the law wasn't close to a physical kingdom, but to a mental state where he was close to God.
   - When he tells his followers to take up their cross and follow him, Jesus says "some who are standing here will not taste death before they see that the kingdom of God has come with power" (Mark 9:1 NIV). Jesus knew that no physical kingdom would come about in the lifetime of anyone present, but this suggests that the kingdom would be present inside his disciples and followers.
   [12 marks available — see p.75 for mark scheme]

Pages 62-63 — People Disregarded by Society

1. Leprosy *[1 mark]*
2. Perfume *[1 mark]*
3. - Some people saw illness and disability as punishments from God, so sick and disabled people were seen as sinners.
   - Some diseases were believed to be passed on by touching, so people suffering from them were isolated to protect others.
   - Some diseases were thought to make people ritually unclean, so they couldn't worship God, and other people wouldn't touch them because they were afraid of becoming unclean too.
   [2 marks available, 1 mark for each correct point]
4. - In the first century, people believed that the symptoms the boy had meant he was possessed by an evil spirit. The boy's father asked Jesus to help his son by driving out the spirit. Some modern Christians believe that this is what really happened to the boy.
   - In the modern day, we know that the boy's symptoms suggest that he had epilepsy. Many modern Christians believe that Jesus cured this disease rather than driving out a spirit.
   [4 marks available — see p.75 for mark scheme]
5. He told everyone what had happened *[1 mark]*.
6. - In the first century, Jews and non-Jews (like this woman who was "a Greek, born in Syrian Phoenicia" (Mark 7:26 NIV)) did not mix, and Gentiles were sometimes discriminated against. Jesus ignored this fact and healed the Gentile woman's daughter anyway. Modern Christians interpret this to mean that they should follow Jesus's example and treat all people equally.
   - At first, Jesus was reluctant to heal the woman's daughter, comparing Jews and Gentiles to "children" and "dogs" (Mark 7:27 NIV). However, she showed that she had faith, and so he healed the girl. This story teaches modern Christians the importance of faith in Jesus.
   - The woman calls Jesus "Lord" (Mark 7:28 NIV) even though she has never met him before. This shows that even Gentiles were starting to recognise the divinity of Jesus, so Christians can come from any background as long as they accept Jesus as the Son of God.
   [5 marks available — see p.75 for mark scheme]
7. Arguments that support the statement:
   - During his life, Jesus spent a lot of time with the poor, the sick and other outcasts from society. If this wasn't a major part of his teaching, he would have spent this time with others instead.
   - Jesus himself said that the most important commandment was "Love your neighbour as yourself" (Mark 12:31 NIV). This would have been hardest when it came to the poor and the sick, so it shows that Jesus's treatment of the poor and the sick is the most important part of his teaching.
   - Even people who don't believe in the Christian God, like some atheists, might agree that Jesus was a very moral man — just not the Son of God. They might also agree that people should follow his example about how to treat the poor and the sick. This part of his teaching is the most important because it relates to everyone, not just to Christians.
   - The protection of the poor and the sick, through a free healthcare system and benefits, is part of modern British society so it's clear that this part of Jesus's teaching has had a huge effect on the world.
   Arguments against the statement:
   - Jesus spent a long time teaching people about the kingdom of God, and how people can get there. Treating the poor and the sick with compassion is only part of Jesus's teaching on how humans can enter the kingdom of God, so it cannot be the most important part of his teaching.

- As well as the poor and sick, Jesus spent a lot of time with sinners like prostitutes and tax collectors — for example, he chose Levi to be his disciple. This suggests that his treatment of other outcasts from society is equally important.
- When Jesus was asked to heal the paralysed man, he instead forgave his sins, only healing him afterwards. This suggests that forgiving people's sins was a more important part of Jesus's teaching than improving their physical health.
[12 marks available — see p.75 for mark scheme]

Pages 64-65 — Faith and Discipleship
1   She had faith *[1 mark]*
2   Walk on water *[1 mark]*
3   Andrew, Peter (Simon Peter), James, John
    [2 marks available, 1 mark for each correct point]
4   - It shows that anyone can lose their faith. Peter was one of Jesus's closest disciples, and if he can betray Jesus, anyone is capable of it. It shows how difficult it is to keep faith and that Christians need God's help to do it.
    - In contrast, Peter's failure is an example of how we all may fail. However, it is an opportunity for Peter to repent and be forgiven and it demonstrates to us the extent of God's forgiveness, showing us that all sins can be forgiven.
    [4 marks available — see p.75 for mark scheme]
5   Pupil *[1 mark]*
6   - To become a disciple, Jesus said that people must "deny themselves and take up their cross and follow me" (Mark 8:34 NIV). This shows Christians that being true followers of Jesus will require sacrifice and suffering.
    - The word 'disciple' means pupil or apprentice. Jesus acted as a teacher, teaching his pupils about the kingdom of God. This shows Christians that they need to study religion and keep trying to understand their faith and God better.
    - When Jesus called the first disciples, Peter and Andrew, they immediately "left their nets and followed him" (Mark 1:18 NIV). This teaches Christians that nothing is more important than following Jesus, not even everyday life or a career.
    - In Mark 16, Jesus sent his disciples out to other towns to preach the Gospel, convert people by baptising them and perform miracles. This shows Christians that they should spend time preaching the Gospel to others, and that they can do miraculous things if they have faith in Jesus.
    [5 marks available — see p.75 for mark scheme]
7   Arguments that support the statement:
    - In John's Gospel, Jesus says "My Father's house has many rooms" (John 14:2 NIV). Some Christians believe that this means there is room in heaven for people of different religions, and that Christianity is not the only way to heaven.
    - Some Christians argue that although the commissioning of the disciples at the end of Mark's Gospel suggests that only Christians will go to heaven, the verses where this took place (verses 9-20) are not included in the original copies of the text.
    - Some Christians argue that much of Jesus's teaching was about how wrong it was to reject people, and that we should love our neighbours as ourselves. They believe that this means good people would not be rejected from heaven just because they are not Christians.
    Arguments against the statement:
    - In order to be saved and go to heaven, people must ask for their sins to be forgiven. This requires a belief in Jesus — John says that Jesus died so "whoever believes in him shall not perish but have eternal life" (John 3:16 NIV). To believe that Jesus was resurrected and can forgive sins means that you are a Christian.
    - Jesus commissioned his disciples to go and preach the Gospel, saying "Whoever believes and is baptised will be saved, but whoever does not believe will be condemned" (Mark 16:16 NIV). This suggests that only those who have been baptised as Christians can be saved and go to heaven.

- Christians believe that sin entered the world when Adam and Eve disobeyed God in Genesis. As a result, all humans are born with 'original sin'. The only way of being redeemed of this sin is through Jesus. This means that all people need to be redeemed by Jesus's death and resurrection, but only Christians who believe in him can be saved.
[12 marks available — see p.75 for mark scheme]

Marking Guidance and Practice
Page 67 — 2 Mark Questions
Answer 2
This answer gets 2 marks out of 2 because it contains two correct points. Point 2) only gets 1 mark, despite giving two facts, because a maximum of 2 marks can be given in total.
Answer 3
This answer gets 1 mark out of 2 because only point 2) is correct. Point 1) is about a form of private Christian worship, but the question is about Islam.

Page 69 — 4 Mark Questions
Answer 1
This answer gets 4 marks out of 4 because two contrasting, relevant points are made about beliefs towards animal experimentation. Each belief is supported by a sufficiently detailed explanation which accurately refers to relevant and specific religious beliefs.
Answer 2
This answer gets 2 marks out of 4 because the first point is relevant, reasonably accurate and has a sufficiently detailed explanation for two marks. The second point, about how Muslims would slaughter animals humanely for food, is not relevant to the question (which is about animal experimentation and not just the treatment of animals). So that point cannot be awarded any marks.

Page 71 — 5 Mark Questions
Answer 1
This answer gets 3 marks out of 5 because two points are made, which are relevant to the question. The points given are simple explanations and so do not get the additional marks for development. A relevant Christian teaching is referred to in the first paragraph, giving the third mark.
Answer 2
This answer gets 5 marks out of 5 because two relevant religious beliefs are given and developed sufficiently, gaining two marks for each paragraph. The quote in the first paragraph satisfies the requirement for a reference to a specific teaching or sacred text, gaining the final mark.

Pages 73-74 — 12 Mark Questions
Answer 1
This answer gets 6 marks out of 12 because there is recognition of different viewpoints in relation to the question. Each paragraph contains some relevant supporting evidence, such as the comparison between Jesus and a sacrificial lamb in the first paragraph, but this is not developed any further. There is clear reference to religion throughout, but the references are general in nature and not specific to this question. There is no conclusion at the end or attempt to evaluate the points made.
Answer 2
This answer gets 12 marks out of 12 because two relevant and opposing viewpoints are laid out clearly, with thorough explanations. There is clear reference to Christian teachings throughout, and the teachings are focused in relation to the question. Each paragraph is well developed, showing a chain of reasoning to support the point being made. There is an evaluation and conclusion made in the final paragraph which relates back to the answer and shows a strong understanding of the topic.

Answers